# On Education for Teacher Educators

# On Education for Teacher Educators

**Padma Satakopachari**
M.Sc.,Ph.D.
*Former Dean*
Faculty of Home Science
M.S. University of Baroda
Baroda.

***Foreword***

**Dr. L.S. Saraswathi**
M.Sc.,Ph.D. (Iowa State University, USA)
*Consultant*
NFE & Education for Development
Tamilnadu.

**NEELKAMAL PUBLICATIONS PVT. LTD.**
**EDUCATIONAL PUBLISHERS**
**(EXPORTERS & IMPORTERS)**
**NEW DELHI HYDERABAD**

# ON EDUCATION FOR TEACHER EDUCATORS

**Padma Satakopachari**

*Foreword*

**Dr. L.S. Saraswathi**



**Edition : 2020**



**ISBN : 978-81-8316-177-0**

**NEELKAMAL PUBLICATIONS PVT. LTD.**
Sultan Bazar, Hyderabad - 500 095.
✆ 24757140, 24757197, +91 80199-18182, +91 91210-01237

***Delhi Office:***
\# 4764/1, 23, Ansari Road, Daryaganj, New Delhi-110 002,
✆ 011-23244237, +91 98118-28953
e-mail : neelkamalbooks@gmail.com
website : www.neelkamalbooks.com

Published by ***Suresh Chandra Sharma*** for
***Neelkamal Publications Pvt. Ltd.,*** New Delhi, Hyderabad
and printed at ***NKPL,*** New Delhi, India.

## Dr. L.S. Saraswathi

M.Sc.,Ph.D. (Iowa State University, USA)
*Consultant*
NFE & Education for Development
Tamilnadu.

It is believed that **Education** provides strength and resilience to people to respond to changing situations and enables them to contribute to **societal development,** which includes **economic development** for furthering the material well being of people; **social and political development** for living harmoniously and promoting a democratic and just society; and **intellectual, cultural and aesthetic development** for enrichment of quality of life. Thus, education is seen as a powerful tool for societal development. The teacher development and empowerment are critical for education to serve these purposes.

Though the professional preparation of teachers at the school level has been recognized as critically important, the significance of professional teacher education for college teachers was hardly given any consideration as it was believed that they are mere transmitters of information and only their subject expertise is important for them to be effective teachers.

Though the need for professional teacher education for college teachers is increasingly recognized the ground reality remains a matter of grave concern.

The present book **"On Education for Teacher Educators"** is timely and sets a meaningful beginning in academic quality enhancement of teachers as professionals at the college level irrespective of the subject areas they teach. With decades of experience in college teaching as teacher educator, as administrator holding key positions in college/university education, the author expresses her genuine concerns regarding the professional competency (in teaching) of the 'community of teachers' at the college level and makes her sincere efforts to crystallize her knowledge, attitudes and skills with regard to teacher education and recording them systematically for the benefit of teacher educators of college teachers to use as a textbook, a guide book and also as a reference volume.

The book brings out the importance of professional education for teaching in colleges and universities and focuses on the conceptual understanding of the educational process for the teacher educators to be reflective and active in their day-to-day educational practice. The context is presented in Chapter I as issues related to the quality of higher education in India. The book elaborates the steps in curriculum planning and implementation in well-structured six chapters. As a base for curriculum planning, the need for developing a philosophy of education is underlined for which the indigenous philosophical ideas are indicated to be of immense importance and a set of guidelines for such a curriculum is provided in Chapter II and in Appendix I. On the basis of the philosophy of education the actual curriculum planning process is explained in Chapters III, IV and V. This included:

- setting goals for curriculum taking into account the contemporary life, the learners and the subject specialists;
- looking at models of nature of professional competency based on the defined constituents of teacher competency;
- examining nature of knowledge, skills and values, as they are crucial components of learning abilities;
- analyzing the aspects of curriculum;
- understanding the role of learning experiences, evaluation and research in developing the curriculum.

Various factors involved in the implementation process of the planned curriculum, especially the processes of providing learning experiences, motivation in the Teacher Education

Programme, communication, management and teaching are presented in Chapter VI.

Special mention should be made of the tremendous efforts made by the author in preparing lists of references and bibliography of readings of both Indian and western authors. It will surely be of immense value to the teacher educators.

Elaborate Appendices especially the one on areas of concern for inclusion in a curriculum for teacher education could well serve as a guideline for curriculum planners and teacher educators.

The style and language of presentation are lucid and simple.

This publication is sure to take forward efforts in professional teacher education of college teachers by all those concerned.

*– Dr. L.S. Saraswathi*

# Preface

There has been a longstanding belief among academics in higher education that expertise in the subject field is sufficient to be effective in their respective subjects. Subject experts have felt that no special knowledge of education apart from expertise in a subject is necessary and that subject specialists by virtue of their scholarship know how to teach their subjects.

However, increasing knowledge of how people learn and of the socio-psychological foundations of the educative process brought to the fore the need and importance of such knowledge in the teaching process. Consequently, a demand arose for teachers of higher education who were acquainted with the subject of education for developing their competency as educators, and not merely as dispensers of factual information. This made teacher education a crucial factor in improving higher education.

Scholarship in the subject of education is not a requirement for teaching in colleges and universities at the time of writing this text. But there are indications in the current public debates on educational issues and in literature that there is recognition of a need for requiring college teachers to be proficient in the subject of education. It has been even suggested that some general courses in Education be introduced as an integral part of undergraduate and postgraduate studies, and intensive courses in Education for those who opt for teaching. Hopefully, there will be a demand in the near future for educators who would be preparing college teachers proficient in the educative process.

It is in the above context that writing this text was undertaken. The aim of this text is to induce some interest in teacher educators in becoming professionally competent educators. The contents of this text are expected to be useful to teacher educators in general and encourage them to read professional literature on Education.

Every attempt has been made to make this text easily readable, helpful in gaining a deeper understanding of the task of preparing college teachers, and in forming a sound concept of the elements involved in the educational process. The emphasis in the contents of this text is on the concepts embedded in the educational process, and not on standard traditional statements of rules, laws and recipes to be used in teaching. The language of the text has been kept as simple as possible by using only necessary professional and technical vocabulary.

It is hoped that reading this as a general text will put the readers at ease with the subject of Education. To encourage further reading of published literature on educational issues, a long list of relevant reading material is presented as 'readings' at the end of a chapter on a section of a chapter. A note explaining the purpose and the nature of the 'readings' list is appended preceding the first chapter. Detailed extracts. reference notes and charts are given as appendices so that the main text could be brief.

Effort has been made to prepare readings lists because access to contemporary thought of scholarly writing is limited in colleges and universities due to limited funds for libraries as well as limited publications of periodicals and books on education in India. These constraints have been faced by the author of this text too. However, in the course of this last decade several publications of books and periodical literature have appeared offering a fairly wide range of reading material on Education, which have been introduced in a large measure in the text with the view of making the readers aware of the excellent educational literature available for more intensive studies.

An outline of areas of curriculum content with an indigenous base for education of college teachers as educators, identified from publications on Teacher Education, is presented in appendix IV. It is hoped that teacher educators will acquaint themselves with these areas of curriculum content, and select content to include in their programmes of education for prospective college teachers. The curriculum content presented in the appendix is meant to serve only as a source of information for preparing particular curricula according to the socio-educational contexts for which the teacher education programs are prepared.

Also, an attempt has been made to show how a curriculum plan can be made operational through an illustration of a plan for teaching the initial unit for motivating interest in students in the teacher education program (Appendix VIII). These efforts should hopefully encourage teacher educators to plan units in teacher education in indigenous contexts, undertake testing of educational hypothesis and teaching strategies, and contribute to the field of teacher education in India. Though the text was written with the college teachers of home science in mind and sporadic references are made to home science education, the contents of this text are applicable to teacher educators in general.

There are six chapters of about ten pages on an average, with eight appendices of varying lengths for further enrichment of text.

I am deeply grateful to Dr. Amrik Singh for sparing his valuable time to scrutinise the text and suggesting some useful additional information to be included. My grateful thanks are due to Sri M.T. Perumal for patiently doing the computer typing of the text pages and preparing duplicates, following carefully the format according to the author's instructions, and also preparing xeroxed copies of the text. Only the author should be held responsible for whatever defects may be found in the text.

– *Padma Satakopachari*

# A Note on the List of Selected Readings after each Chapter

A list of relevant reading materials is given at the end of each chapter for gaining a more comprehensive and deeper understanding of the topics discussed in the chapter. It is hoped that the reading lists will encourage teacher educators to read professional literature on education, find the subject of education intellectually and emotionally challenging, and inspire teacher educators to improve their teacher education programs.

A large number of readings are presented since availability of publications may be limited in each educational institution, and so that there is scope for choosing suitable reading material. The list of sources of cited references in the text may also be added to the list of readings. From this list teacher educators may select their own reading material for their own enrichment and also select required reading material for students in the course of study planned in their programme of teacher education.

No doubt that good reading material will continue to be published that teacher educators need to he aware of so that the lists presented here are pruned and enriched by deletions and additions for keeping in tune with educational developments and changed circumstances. Information on books can be gathered from book reviews and publications of the UGC. the Association of Indian Universities, NCERT, National Institute of Educational Planning and Administration, literary supplements of newspapers, catalogues of publications of universities and catalogues of publications of book publishers. Book publishers of repute may also send catalogues free of cost to teachers in universities for their publicity or on request.

Teacher educators need to constantly scan catalogues and reviews of publications on education to select books to read and bring up-to-date their professional knowIedge. The cutting edge of knowledge on education can be found in journal and newspaper articles and in research papers of universities in university libraries. The lists presented in the text are not exhaustive as publications on education in the form of articles are too voluminous to be listed fully, even if only those relevant to a specific topic are selected. Also, ideas and information are in general repeated by several writers so that a list of the size given here maybe assumed to be representative of publications in the last decade of the twentieth century on the topics in the text.

The limited access to publications or libraries accounts for the narrow range of the sources of literature on education presented in the reading lists. The reading lists should be regarded only as the base line for teachers building up their own library of references, widening the range of sources of publications referred to for selecting articles to read.

Except from the point of view of relevance to the topic of a chapter, including an article in the reading list is not an evaluation of the quality of the material as the quality is presumed to be acceptable as judged by the editors and publishers who had published it. Teacher educators need to read these references and evaluate them with an open. informed and a critical mind The articles on education are generally broad in their coverage of' educational aspects so that different parts of an article may be pertinent to topics in different chapters and not relevant in its entirety to only one chapter.

On Education for Teacher Educators

# Contents

❖ ❖ ❖

# Introduction

A brief account of the historical background that shaped the educational system of India and the views of scholars on the present status of higher education in India are presented in this chapter. This also serves to give the rationale and justification for exploring new approaches to the preparation of college teachers that teacher educators need to think about. It is important for teacher educators to know what factors affected the higher educational system in India.

# Section 1 State of Higher Education in India

Even before India attained independence in 1947 and also afterwards, dissatisfaction with the quality and functioning of the educational system of the country was expressed by educationists, statesmen, social reformers and eminent citizens.[1] Especially, in the closing decades of the Twentieth century , caustic derogatory comments were made by the concerned public through the mass media on the quality of education in the universities and colleges of India. The quality of university teachers too came in for severe criticism in published literature on higher education. Abundant literature, too numerous to list for reference here, continue to be published deploring in strong terms the falling standards of higher education.[2]

The major Education Commissions of the Ministry of Education of the Government of India, in 1948–49 and 1964–66, pointed out the shortcomings of higher education in India.[3] The Education Commission of 1966 had this to say about the falling standards in the quality of education

> ... it is difficult to say definitely to what extent and in what respects they have been falling. What is however apparent and really matters is that over a large area of education the content and quality are inadequate for our present needs and future requirements.[4]

Saraf, after reviewing seven Five Year Plans, the documents of 1946, 1968, and 1986, and The National Policy on Education stated

> This synoptic presentation of policies and programmes incorporated in the first seven plans indicates conclusively that several reforms and innovations have been repeated and re-emphasised over time in one form or the other. Sometimes one wonders whether, in spite of massive investments made over the years, there has been any major qualitative change in the state of general university education since the attainment of independence in 1947.[5]

Employers in industries and commerce, and in institutions of public service pointed out through various media of communication the. lack of competence in the graduates for the jobs for which they applied. A research study showed that in the case of' home science graduates they lacked competence for the jobs they held as perceived by their employees.[6] A majority of home science graduates were found to be employed in teaching and research, their competence forming a significant source of human resource greatly required for national development. Hence their incompetence became a matter of concern.

Innumerable writings of eminent educators, social reformers and political leaders indicated that the need of the hour was change in the quality of the education given in universities. A qualitative change in higher education can come about only when universities and colleges have teachers who are competent in bringing about qualitative changes in the educational system. Such competence requires an understanding of the social change processes, their implications for education, and the. potential and scope of the educational processes to help bring about the needed social change. But as Srivastava complained whatever changes in the educational system took place they were superficial, and showed only structural changes, while teaching methods remained the same. He gave examples of structural changes as rearranging courses in different patterns, discarding numerical marks for letters, and replacing 'terms' by 'semesters'.[7]

It has become almost a maxim on the importance of the quality of teachers that the quality of citizens in a country depended on the quality of their education, and the quality of education in turn depended on the quality of teachers.[8]

Yet the question of the education of teachers of higher education received very little attention from the planners of educational policy on educational reforms. This lacuna in educational reforms appears to be due to the general belief that very little pedagogic element is involved in teaching youth at the college level. The Education Commission of 1966 reported that no provisions were made for the professional initiation of a university teacher and that the tradition in India has been to regard training for college teaching as unnecessary.[9]

Academicians in general seem to have held the view that universities and colleges were not to be held responsible for students who were old enough to learn by themselves. This situation continued till the last decade of the twentieth century, as pointed out by Rajamony and Saravanan:

> As far as higher education is concerned, many in the higher ups thought there was no need for training teachers at the higher educational level. This is no more valid as in any kind of activity including teaching in universities and colleges training of teachers will certainly be beneficial for providing better education for students.[10]

Three years later a similar statement was made by Kumar.[11] Stressing the importance of the role played by university staff in the performance of universities, Rastogi stated that adequate attention was seldom paid to the preparation, training and upgrading of both academic and administrative staff.[12]

Sharma and Sharma, said that the spirit of professionalism was gradually disappearing in the country, and it was more evident in the teaching profession. As a result the quality of education was greatly affected and in spite of various commissions and new educational policies, the standard of education was gradually falling. For this, though there may have been various factors responsible, poor professionalism among teachers was an evident reason.[13]

So far, the deterioration of educational standards of higher education and the quality of college and university teachers in India have been discussed. For a more comprehensive view of the state of higher education it is necessary to look at the effort made by the Government of India to improve the quality of higher education in this country. A special apex body known as the University Grants Commission (UGC) was established in 1956. What effort was made by the UGC and how they were effective in improving the quality of higher education, extensively studied and discussed in published educational literature, is presented in the following pages.*

From 1961 onwards the UGC gave grants to universities for organizing symposia, summer schools, and refresher courses. After the Kothari Commission Report of 1966, the UGC started orientation courses for new and junior faculty for a week in every college. Joshi and Singh, in a survey of 113 colleges and universities in 1978, found that only eighteen universities gave some sort of training for own staff and reported that the performance of the orientation courses were dismal.[14] Refresher courses were initiated by the UGC from 1960 onwards and extended through (1969 to 1972) throughout the country. Recommendations made on the basis of evaluation of these courses between 1967 and 1972 received very little support from universities, the courses being almost given up in the seventies.[15]

Though Academic Staff Colleges were set up in 1986 by the UGC for conducting pre-service training and refresher courses, no review was done even by 1993 as to how teachers utilized the

* The following pages are based on information gathered after studying 16 articles specifically referring to UGC initiated programmes, out of 113 articles on teacher education in higher education in periodicals such as the University News, the Journal of Higher Education, the Journal of Educational Planning and Administration, as well as relevant chapters in books on higher education, published between 1990 and 2005.

programmes of the 47 ASCs.[16] Out of twenty-two writers who evaluated the performance of the ASCs, seventeen were dissatisfied[17] with the ASC programmes, and it was doubted if the ASCs would be of any use to teacher educators, as a coherent policy and programme for professional development was absent.[18] Six major deficiencies that made these courses unsatisfactory were pointed out.[19]

From 1970, the UGC sponsored seminars, summer institutes, pre-service and in-service orientation, refresher courses, university leadership, research and study leave. Evaluation of these programmes made between the years 1983–1988 by the National Commission On Teaching showed that participation in these programmes was less than three-fourths the number of college and university teachers, and a quarter of the number of college teachers availed of the study leave scheme.[20]

Commenting on the role and functioning of the UGC, Amrik Singh questioned "to what extent the UGC utilised the powers of coordination and determination of the standards vested in it," and said "the simplest answer would be that had these powers been put to use even partially, the situation in higher education would not have been what it is today." He argued that in spite of social and political compulsions the UGC had a professional and a feasible role to play, and that was "the role of setting and upholding the norms and standards of high quality education in universities. Failing to perform this role the UGC remained predominantly a grant giving body.[21] quantitative expansion was fully utilized while those meant for qualitative improvement lapsed to the extent of fifty percent.[22]

In 1995, Chalam pointed out that it was yet to be assessed as to what extent the upgrading of the pay-scales of university teachers, as recommended by the Mehrotra Committee in 1980, attracted the top talent to the educational system, and to what extent it improved the quality of higher education. He felt that quality related issues in higher education could he tackled by strengthening the recruitment mechanism.[23] After 1989, to strengthen the recruitment mechanism, a mandatory National Eligibility test (NET) to qualify for college and university teaching was introduced. This teaching was commented upon as not making even fifty percent of postgraduates effective as teachers.[24] The UGC was charged with shifting its stand from time to time as to whom to exempt from this test. The UGC agreed in 2006 to exempt the M.Phil. and the Ph.D. degree holders from this, test, thus equating higher qualifications in subject fields with eligibility to teach.[25]

A more professional effort was made in 1994 by establishing the National Assessment and Accreditation Council that called for voluntary participation by universities in self-appraisal. After a slow takeoff in the following first decade[26], thanks to the UGC's repeated intentions to favour only the accredited institutions, by 2005 the NAAC's accreditation programme seemed to be working.[27]

The UGC tried to improve higher education from the angle of examination reforms, seeing the need for it, as the whole of higher educational system was being wagged by the degree examinations as reported by several authors of educational articles.[28] A review of the UGC's reforms in 1977 by the Education Department showed that several panels on examination reforms worked for more than a decade until a working group under the Ministry of Education made a Plan of Action in 1971 which was circulated in 1973, for universities to implement.[29] A follow-up scheme was introduced to help university teachers to improve assessment of learning by students by setting valid and reliable question papers. Accordingly, universities formed committees with external and internal experts for framing a large number of questions, exhaustive of the prescribed syllabus, building up a 'question bank'. The teachers would then be able to select valid and reliable questions for their question papers. These questions could be scrutinized on the basis of responses from students and improved, thus improving the quality of examinations. "But these improvements have not removed the major defects of the examination system."[30] The idea of internal assessment to counter the uncertainties of terminal external examinations was also resisted by both students and teachers, the former fearing bias and victimization by teachers and the latter disliking additional work and loss of examination paper setting and evaluation fees.

Several conditions were seen to impinge upon teachers of universities and colleges that lead to their indifference and apathy towards working for change and improvement of the quality of higher education.[31] The lack of a mindset for change has been pointed out.[32] In the words of Amrik Singh "it is not going to he easy to persuade the teachers to perform better. The operative word here is 'persuade'. Teachers cannot be ordered about"[33].

Many educators for the past two decades have exhaustively dealt with the deficiencies of India's higher educational system and made valuable suggestions for reforms. However. the situations described in the foregoing pages indicate that, along with the ongoing efforts, there is a need for an approach that will help teachers help themselves in their professional tasks. The following sections and chapters exemplify this approach. The main thrust in this text is to build a positive self-image of the teacher as a crucial player in developing through education the human resources that are vital to national development, to instil a professional pride in being an effective teacher, and to promote the self-confidence that comes from understanding the key concepts of the educational process and procedures.

# Need and Importance of Education for Teaching in Colleges and Universities

Several educators increasingly emphasized the need for educating teachers for teaching at the college and university levels. Nearly every week the major daily newspapers, and almost every issue of professional periodical journals, directly or indirectly concerned with the educational system of this country, carried articles on the importance of professional competence of teachers in the task of educating youth in higher education.

The Report of the Education Commission of 1966, while accep-ting that there are born teachers who win over the respect of students by their scholarship and dedication, held that the bulk of teachers did not fall into this category, and needed some training and orientation to the teaching profession.[34] Following are some of the opinions quoted from articles in journals and newspapers on the importance of the professional competence of teachers in higher education.

> ... improving the quality of education through the process of upgrading the input; is an undeniable key issue today. The single dominant input that can influence quality is the 'teacher. It is only in this context that several committees in the past pointed out the need to improve the status of teachers.[35]

In the opinion of Trivedi "Respect for the worth of knowledge in our context, and especially in professional education preparing educators is a matter which deserves immediate consideration"[36]

According to Bawa, teacher education will assume greater importance in the coming years, because, firstly, larger number of teachers will need to be trained for meeting increasing demand, and secondly, teacher education will be under considerable pressure to provide teachers capable of imparting quality education.[37]. Mehrotra commented in an article that the need for some type of pedagogical training was being felt rather strongly since I950.[38]

Pointing out that appraisal of teacher competence was a neglected aspect of education, Mani referred to the Kothari Commission of I966, the Sen Comnittee of 1973, the Mehrothra Committee of 1985, and the document the National Policy on Education of 1986, all stressing the need for performance appraisal of teachers and for educating teachers for their profession, if processional competence was to be improved.[39]

Reinforcing the call for improving the quality of teachers, Indiresan had this to say

> ...the teacher is the heart of any educational institution, So, any effort to improve the quality of educational outcomes would depend to a large extent on the quality of its teachers who are the key instruments of change.[40]

On the same lines, Kothari and Rao felt that the need for teacher education programme at college/university is yet to be fully appreciated, and defects in higher education ultimately were likely to give rise to ineffective inputs into secondary/higher secondary teacher education programmes.[41]

In the opinion of Rajput and Walia, we have to develop a cadre of people who consider it a privilege and a challenge to prepare teachers for the country.[42] Though the Central Advisory Board of Education Committee on Policy in 1992 and earlier, the NPERC in 1990, concurred that a one year pre-induction training programme for college and university teachers should be organised, the Policy of Action took no notice of this recommendation.[43] Different educators have suggested different patterns of teacher education programmes for college and university teachers such as pre-service, in-service, orientation, and refresher courses, as well as attendance at seminars, symposia and workshops, throughout the professional life of teachers. Opinions given above are only a few examples from a large volume of writing by educators and educational policy makers on the issue of improving the quality of teachers and teaching in the colleges and universities in India.

"It is imperative on the part of educational planners," say Rajput and Walia, "to develop a national system of teacher education based on India's cultural ethos, its unity and diversities synchronizing its inherent strength and national identity. The system needs to prepare professionally competent teachers... "[44]

It is observed by enlightened educationists that the academic community remains encrusted in the traditional system of education and seems to be paralyzed by apathy, helplessness and hopelessness. A distressing array of opinions of current sociologists, socio-psychologists, and educational philosophers conveys the gigantic task in making changes in the quality of higher education, and the helplessness of academicians and political leaders in this task. Ruhela in 1990, gives a telling example of a forecast of educational stagnation in India in these words:

> The worst that can happen in these circumstances is for one to open the door of a typical classroom in 2000 and walking into it to find the teacher standing up front and talking.[45]

Focus on the need for educating college and university teachers in the science and the art of education, to become a competent educator, emerged clearly only in the last two decades of the twentieth century in this country. Realisation of the crucial role of teacher education and the enormity of the task of preparing teachers who would face challenges in improving the higher educational system reached a climax near the end of the twentieth century, but as yet have not been translated into action. The maladies of higher education continue to be highlighted daily in newspapers and journals.

# Is "Education" or "Training" Needed for College Teachers?

Mostly in published literature on preparation of teachers, the term used is 'training' of teachers. This term as used by many educators, does not appear to imply that any discrimination exists between the concept of 'training' and of 'education', and leads one to doubt if these concepts are discriminated by many educators. In India most of the suggestions by educators, administrators, and interested academicians are for introduction of specific topics, curriculum modules, audio-visual devices, and procedural strategies in the teacher education curriculum for 'training' teachers. Such suggestions are suitable to the definition of 'training', which according to Tyler, refers to a narrow form of education focusing on attaining a high level of skill in performance.

Tyler distinguished between the concepts of 'training' and 'education' as follows:

> One can think of two kinds of learning, one we call 'training' and the other 'education'. Training is the kind of learning where the total pattern is given and the learner follows precisely what has been taught. This we call narrowing the span of behaviour of the learner so that he performs just like the teacher. Then there is education where there is emphasis upon trying to open doors, making it possible for the person to do many more than he did before and to keep opening doors so that he is learning all the time. Professional people need to be educated and not trained.[46]

The distinction between 'training' and 'education' is all the more important when the social environment in which the universities and colleges of India have been functioning has been changing along with rapidly changing social, economic and political changes in the country. Due to a narrow concept of 'training' teachers the educational system of India has not been responsive to the social and economic changes, and consequently, has been out of gear with life outside the campuses. On the other hand the preparation of university and college teachers should include the study of the discipline of education to promote an understanding of the challenges faced by higher education in India.

Also, the curriculum of teacher education should reflect the goals, norms and challenges described in the documents on the National Policy of Education published by the Government of India in 1985 and 1986, and enable teachers to become competent to cope with these.[47]

From 1986 onwards the University Grants Commission introduced a regulation requiring applicants to teaching posts in colleges and universities to pass an examination for teaching in colleges, set by the Indian Council of Scientific Research and the Indian Council of Social Science Research. This was a measure brought in to secure a minimum level of quality in the new entrants to the teaching profession at the higher educational level. Regrettably this eligibility test did not place emphasis on the subject of 'Education' but on the proficiency of college teachers in their specialization and hence could not be expected to improve the standards of teaching and evaluation by college teachers. Developing the professional competency of university and college teachers as 'educators' needs to be given the highest priority in India's educational policy. Even in 1995, Chalam said "... improving the quality of education through the process of upgrading the inputs is an undeniable key issue today". The single dominant input that can influence quality is the 'teacher'.[48]

## 3.1 The Special Challenge in the Education of Home Science College Teachers

Chandrasekar stated that the crucial need in home science was for a large number of well qualified teachers who in turn can train teachers for school and extension services.[49] Improving teacher education is a prerequisite to improving the quality of education at any level.

It is being increasingly realized that the key element in an educational programme is the curriculum. Increasingly, the focus of the present literature in teacher education is on developing a teacher education curriculum that meets the demand for teachers competent in offering education that satisfies a changing society's needs.

Professional excellence is required for bringing into home science education an element of relevance to the socio-economic realities of the Indian home and family life in relation to the changing social contexts. Standards of excellence should be set for the curriculum of teacher education for home scientists to meet these needs.

If home science is to have indigenous cultural roots, there is a great need to build up research competence for developing content with a scientific and cultural base in India, as also for innovating teaching strategies suitable to the subject and prevailing teaching conditions in our universities. Curriculum development in teacher education should therefore be the foremost issue to be attended to.

# Reference Notes

28 Comments on the examination system by writers on education:

a) "the need of the masses to use education to buy jobs subjects the university and the school system to the pressure of competition in the job market. This led to the unhealthy practice of cramming for examinations for the sake of competitive success. "...the credentialising function of the university progressively replaced any other nobler purpose of education." (Francis Sounderraj. "Schools of Excellence – an Alternative," *The Hindu speaks on Education*, 1997)

b) The over whelming preoccupation of the students is with the passing of examinations, and in the case of the brighter students of attaining a high rank or grade." In such perception of students, the purpose of gaining knowledge for the sake of it or mastering the subject is at a discount. Students who do not study are prepared to go to any extent to get the certificate of passing." They attend coaching classes, resort to unethical practices of copying from answers smuggled in, and even fake certificates of having obtained a degree. "The behavior of teachers add to the indifference of the students "however, such has been the deterioration in the system of higher education that quite a few teachers have interest neither in their own subject nor in their students," (P.R. Dubashi. "Accountability in Universities," *The Hindu Speaks on Education.*)

"The examination reforms have been attempted at the school and at the university level. A lot of reports have been undertaken. Studies have been conducted and doctoral degrees awarded to scholars on how to evaluate learning and conduct examinations effectively, without making these a torture for the examinee. It would not need much effort to visit a university or a school in some remote area to observe that the examinations are still being conducted in the same old fashion as was in vogue decades ago." (J.S. Rajput, " The Teaching Scenario," *The Hindu Speaks on Education.*)

31 Conditions impinging upon teachers leading to their indifference: corrosive political system: too much importance to research and publications; closed or direct (autocratic) organisational climate, reward structure militating against genuine, silent, and self respecting teachers, as careerism and sycophancy is rewarded, pushing back creativity and excellence; the utilitarian and pragmatic milieu of the larger society affect teachers' values; bureaucritisation and comemercialization of education prompt mechanical and money centered attitude; increasing use of media constrict teachers' concern with students; the touch and feel of human contact gradually vanishing in the classrooms; lack of ability and imagination on the part of administrators to enable teachers to actualize their potentiality." (Umrao Singh Chaudhury, "Underperformance and Indifference of Teachers in higher education.")

## References Cited

### For Section 1

1 a) Keay, F.E., *A History of Education in India and Pakistan*, Chennai: Oxford University Press, 1959, pp. 206, 207.

b) Kabir, Humayan, *Indian Phlilosophy of Education*, Asia Publishing House, Madras, 1961. pp. 197, 198.

3 Government of India, Reports of the Education Commissions of 1948, 1953, and 1966, Publications Division, Ministry of Education: New Delhi.

4 ———. Report of the Education Commission (1966): Education and National Development, Publications Division, Ministry of Education, New Delhi, 1966, p. 278.

5 Saraf, S.N., "Higher Education and Five Year Plans: Policies and Perspectives" in *Higher Educatjpn in India: The Social context* by Amrik Singh and G,D. Sharma (editors), Konark Publishers Private Ltd., Delhi, 1988, pp. 265–286.

6 Saraswathi, L.S., "Jobs Held by Home Scientists and Competencies Required for the Same", *ICSSR Research Abstracts Quarterly* (Vol. V:3 and 4), 1974. p. 161

7 Srivastava, Anand "Some Facets of Faculty Development," *University News,* Vol..XVI:13 (July 1, 1978), Association of Indian Universities, New Delhi, pp. 1015, 1016.

8 Chaudhary, U.S., "Professional Competencies of College Teachers," *University News* (November 6,1989). pp. 6,7.

9 Government of India Report of the Education Commission (1966) *Op.cit.* p. 278

10 Rajamony and Aravanan "Development of a Curriculum for Orientation of University Teachers," *University News* {April 15, 1991), pp. 8–14.

11 Kumar, H. "Faculty Training and Development," *University News*, (August 22, 1994). p. 8.

12 Rastogi, Savita, "Academic Staff Development in Higher Education: Training for Efficiency in Teaching, Research, and Management," Documentation, *Journal of Higher Education* (Vol.22: No.1, Spring, 1999), p. 147.

13 Sharma, A.P. and Usha Sharma. "On Professionalism among Teachers," *University News* (November 30, 1992). p. 5.

14 Rastogi, Savita, "Academic Staff Development in Higher Education," *University News* (April 5, 1997), pp. 5-8.

15 Merhotra, R.C., "Professional Development of Teachers: Orientation: Programmes and Refresher Courses," *University News* (January 4, 1993), p. 9.

16 ———. Ibid.

17 Mohanty, S. B., "Excellence in Training of Higher Education Teachers," *Journal of Higher Education*, Vol. 19, No.1, (Spring 1996), pp. 31-42.

18 Raina, V.K., "Strengthening the Colleges of Teacher Education," *Journal of Higher Education*, Vol. 19, No. 1 , (Spring, 1996), pp. 31–42.

19 Pethe, A., "Increasing the Effectivcncss of Teacher Training – A Fresh Look at the Refresher Courses for College Teachers," *University News*, (September 28, 1998). pp. 8–10.

20 Rastogi, S, *Op. cit.*

21 Amrik Singh, "Foundation and Role of UGC," *Higher Education in India: The Social Context* (eds.) Amrik Singh and G.D. Sharma,

Delhi: Konark Publishes Pvt. Ltd., 1988, pp. 234–251.

[22] Chaudhuri, U.S., “Professional Competence of College Teachers ,” *University News* (November 6, 1989), pp. 6.

[23] Chalam, K.S., “Faculty Recruitment,” *The Hindu*, (October 17,1995 ), p. 26.

[24] Chaudhury, U.S., “Underperformance and Indifference of Teachers in Higher Education,” *University News.*

[25] Mahadevan, G., “Casting Away the NET,” Education Plus, *The Hindu,* May, 29, 2006).

[26] a) Editorial, *The Hindu* (August 16. 1996).

b) Antony, Stella, “A Strategy for Internal Quality Management”, *University News*, (July 26. 1993), pp. 1–4.

[27] Antony, Stella and A.Gnanam. “Making the most of Accreditation: Balancing the National and international Development in Higher Education,” reviewed by S. Bhagavatulla. Journal of Educational Planning and Administration (April, 2005), pp. 281–284.

[28] Reference Notes

[29] Singh, Amrik. “Higher Education in India: Structural and Other Problems,” *University News*, (May, 21, 1990 )

[30] Shaik Mowla, “Reforming the Existing System,” *The Hindu* (12-1 0-1993), p. 19.

[31] Chaudhurv, U.S., *Op. cit.*

[32] Antony and Gnanam, *Op. cit.*

[33] Singh, Amrik, *Higher Education in India : The Social Context*, *Op. cit.*, p. 324.

**For Section 2**

[34] Government of India Education commission (1966), *Op.cit.*, pp. 85, 86.

[35] Chalam, K.S. "Faculty Recruitment – Need for Reorientation," Education Open Page, *The Hindu* (October 17, 1993), p. 26.

[36] Trivedi, R. S. "Indian Education and Educators by 2000 A.D.", *University News* (June 14, 1998). pp. 3,4.

[37] Bawa, M.S. "Reorienting Teacher Education in India," *University News*, (September, 2,1991). p. 8.

[38] Mehrotra, R.C. "Professional Development of Teachers: Orientation Programme and Refresher Courses," *University News* (January, 4, 1993), p. 9.

[39] Mani, Mallika. "A Neglected Aspect," Education: Open Page, *The Hindu* (February, 1991), p. 1.

[40] Indiresan, Jayalakshmi. "Faculty Development: Some Issues and Trends," *University News* (January 14, 1991), p. 29.

[41] Kothari,R.G. and Divakara Rao. "University of Teacher Education," *University News* (March 20, 1995), pp. 11–14.

[42] Rajput, J.S. and K. Walia. "Quality Teachers for Future," *Journal of Higher Education* (Vol.22:1, Spring. 1999), p.116.

[43] Kothari and Rao *Op. cit.*

[44] Rajput and Walia *Op. cit.*, p. 117.

[45] Ruhela, S.P. "Teacher Education in India: Futurological Perspectives." *University News,* (May 28, 1990), p. 1.


**For Section 3**


[46] Tyler, R.W. "Concepts, Skills,Values and Curriculum Development", a mimeograph copy of talk given at a conference on "Extension Curriculum Development" Washington, D.C., January, 1963.

[47] Government of India. Documents, 1) The Challenge of Education: A Policy Perspective (1985), 2) A Conceptual Framework to Shape

| | |
|---|---|
| | the National Policy in Education and the Programme of Action (1986). |
| [48] Chalarn, K.S. | "Faculty Recruitment: the Need for Reorientation," Open Page; Education, *The Hindu* (October 17, 1995). |
| [49] Chandrasekhar, Maragatham | Inaugural Address: Proceedings of the Seventh Biennial Conference of the HSAI, October 19–22, 1964. |

# List of Readings

Books, Articles and Research Papers
Relevant to Chapter 1 on the State of Higher Education in India


## BOOKS

**Atma Ram.** *India – 50 years of Independence 1947-97: Status, Growth and Development 5: Education,* Delhi: B.R. Publishing Corporation, 1995.

**Avari, J.W.** *College Education in India.* P.C. Manaktalas and Sons Pvt. Ltd.Bombay, 1967.

**Chauhan, C.P.S.** *Higher Education in India: Achievements, Failures and Strategies*, Aashish Publishing House, 1990.

**Ghosh, Suresh Chandra.** *The History of Education in Modern India*, 1757–1998, Chennai: Orient Longman.

**Keay, F.E.** *A History of Education in India and Pakistan*, Chennai: Oxford University Press. 1959.

**Mathur, Y.B.** *Women's Education in India (1813–1966)*, Bombay: Asia Publishing House, 1973, pp.1–17.

**Moonis Raza (ed.).** *Higher Education in India: Retrospect and Prospect*, Delhi: Vikas Publishing Company, 1990.

**Mukherji, S.N.(ed.)** *Administration of Education in India*, Baroda: Acharya Book Depot, 1967, pp.1–18.

**Panchamukhi, P.R. (ed.)** *Perspectives for Education Reforms in India*, Bombay Himalaya ,1989.

**Raj, K.N.** *Crisis of Higher Education in India* (Patel Memorial Lectures) Bombay: Botwala Chambers, 1970.

**Sarup, Anand and Sulabha Brahma.** *Planning for the Millions*, Delhi: Wiley Eastern, 1990.

**Shrimali, K.L.** *Problems of Education in India in 1955–1960*, 1961.

**Singh, Amrik and G.D. Sharma (eds.).** *Higher Education in India: The Social Context*, Delhi :Konark Publishers Pvt Ltd., 1988, pp. 1–22, 46–53, and 74–108.

**Vakil, K.S. and S. Natarajan.** *Education in India*, Bombay: Allied Publishers, 1966.

## ARTICLES IN JOURNALS AND NEWSPAPERS

**Ali Mahmood.** "Training of University Teachers – A Strategic Requirement", *University News,* 38:47, (November 20, 2000). pp. 16–18.

**Ambirajan, S.** "The Tragedy of Higher Education," *The Hindu,* (April 17, 1999)

**Arora, G.L.** "Teacher Education at the Cross-roads," *University News*, 36:23, (June 8, 1988). pp.1

**Atma Ram.** "To Work More Effectively," *The Hindu* (August, 1993) "Revamping Teacher Education University" *University News* (November, 25,1996). pp. 29–36.

**Beeby, C.E.** "The Quality of Education in Developing Countries: Quantitative vs. Qualitative Concerns", *Social and Economic Studies* Vol.16:4 (December, 1 967).

**Bhadauria, Mridula.** "Emerging Demands on Teacher Education" *University News*, 38:51 (December 18,2000). pp.7–9.

**Bhat, Vignesh N.** "Higher Education for 21" Century India – A Critical Reflection," *University News*, Vol. 37:31, (August 2, 1999). pp. 6,7, and 10.

**Chalam, K.S.** "The Changing Scenario of Higher Education : Coping with the Challenges in the Twenty first Century," *University News* 41:28 (July 14–20, 2003).

**Chauhan, C.P.S.** "An Innovative Look at Teacher Education," *University News* 37:43 (October 25, 1999). pp. 10,1 1.

**Chittibabu, S.N.** "A Messenger of Faith and Encouragement," Review of *Education in Being a Teacher* by Amrik Singh, *University News* 26, (July 1). pp. 10–22.

**Datta, Amlan.** "The Dilemma of Higher Education," *The Telegraph,* (18-8-'89).

**Datta, Amresh.** "Academic Excellence Matters little in our Universities," *The Times of India* (23-5-'89).

**Dilip,K. Dora and Ashok, K.Nanda.** "Value Crisis of Academics: The Way Out ," *Universily News* Vol.41:22 (June 02-08, 2003).

**Dutt, S.** "The Indian Ethos and Modern Education," *The Hindu* (9-5-'89).

**Gopalan, K.** "Higher Education in India: Prospects and Perspectives," *University News* (January, 9, 1995). pp.1–10.

**Jharta, M. and Jharta, B.** "Education System in India: Problems and Prospects," *University News* (June, 5, 1995). pp. 9–12.

**Kulandaisamy, V.C.** "Higher Education Leads Towards Leadership," excerpts from convocation address at Manonmaniam Sundaranar University, *University News*, 37:39 (September 27, 1999). pp.13–16.

"A Major Challenge," Sub-editorial, *The Hindu* (Saturday, June 29, 1991), pp.1,2.

**Maheshwari, Amarnath.** "Paradigm Shift in Context and Process of Education," Excerpts from Convocation Address of the Sixty-eighth Annual Convocation of Annamalai University, January 10,2001, *University News* 39:18, (April 30,2001). pp. 26–28.

**Marniar, M.** "Recruitment is the Key to Quality," Education, The Open Page, *The Hindu*, (July 5th or 6th, 1990).

**Nath, K.P.** "Education and Socio-economic Development," *University News* (June 14, 1993). pp.1,2.

**Panandikar, Pal.** "Paradox of Unemployment: Failings of the Educational System," The Times of India, (1.5.'89).

**Pandey, Saroj.** "Roadmap to Quality INSET Need based Training," *University News* 37:27, (July 5,1999). pp. 13–20.

**Paul Justin.** "Towards Academic Excellence," *University News* 38:23, (Junes, 2000). pp. 7, 8.

———. "What is Wrong in Academies" *University News* 39:30, (March 26, 2001). pp. 10, 11.

**Prakash, Ohm.** "Higher Education or Tertiary Education?" *University News* (November 5, 1990), pp. 4,5.

**Pylee, M.V.** "Limited but Useful," Review of *Problems of Higher Education in India* by C.M. Ramachandran, *University News* 38, (September 19.1988). pp. 51–54.

**Rajput, J.S.** "Search for Direction in Education," *University News*, 38:21, (May 22, 2000). pp.1–5.

**Ranuchandran, P.** "Public Opinion on Education," *The Indian Journal of Sociology*, Vol. XXXI : 4, (January, 1971 ). pp. 355–356.

**Rao, L.S. Prasad.** "Higher Education in India," Review Essay on *Higher Education in India: The. Social Context*, edited by

Amrik Singh and G.D.Sharma, *University News*, (June 12, 1989). pp. 9–13.

**Rastogi, Savita.** "Academic Staff Development in Higher Education," *University News*, Vol.36:33, (August 17,1998). pp.1–4.

**———.** "Academic Staff Development in Higher Education," *University News* 37:14, (April 5,1999). pp. 5–8.

**Reddy, I.V.** "The Importance of Being a Teacher," *University News* (November 28, 1994). p. 5.

**Ruhela, S.P.** "Teacher Education in India: Futurological Perspectives," *University News* (May, 28, 1990). p. 1.

**Sant, Bharat, R.** "Overcoming, Weaknesses in Higher Education System," *University News* 39:22, (May 28-June 3, 2001). pp.11-12.

**———.** "Towards Achieving Excellence in Higher Education," *University News* 32:19, (May 8, 2000).

**Sarup, Anand.** "Higher Education Needs a New Paradigm," *University News* (January 27, 1992). pp. 1,2.

**Sharma, A.P. and Usha Sharma.** "On Professionalism Among Teachers," *University News* (Novernber,30, 1992). p. 5

**Singh, Amrik.** "The Dismal State of Our Universities," *The Times of India.*

**Singh, Sukhdev and S.K. Mehta.** "Declining Standards of Higher education: A University Teacher's View," *University News.* Vol.37:52, (December 27, 1999). pp. 10–15 and 18.

**Singhvi, L.M.** "The Index of Civilisation," Convocation Address at the 72nd Convocation of Delhi University, *University News.*

**Sounderraj, H. Francis.** "Twentieth Century Changes and 'Their Challenges to Higher Education in India," *University News*, (November 5, 1970). pp. 1–3.

"The State of Universities," Editorial, *The Tribune* 5-5-'89.

**Srinivas, G.** "SWOT Analysis of Higher Education," *University News*, 38:48, (November 27, 2000). pp.1–3.

**Suryanaravanan, M.** "Hurdles in Higher Education," *Deccan Herald*, 10-8-'89.

**Tilak, Jandhyala, B.G.** "Higher Education Reform in India," *University News*, 36:44. (November 2, 1998). pp. 1–7. (Same article also in *JL of Higher Education*, (Spring, 1999).

**Uberoi, I.R.** "Higher education: The Fate of Commissions and Committees: A Lesson for the Twenty-first Century," *Journal of Higher Edcation*, Vol. 18:3 (Monsoon 1995). pp. 485–494.

**Vandan Mohad and Veena,V. Mohad.** "Crisis in Higher Education: Causes and Remedies" *University News*, Vol.41:21, (May 26–June 01, 2003).

# Developing a Curriculum in Teacher Education for College Teachers

Many approaches to curriculum development have been postulated by countries of the West such as the United States, Canada, United Kingdom, Germany and France. These countries have had the experience of planning higher education for nearly a century before India's independence, and have put forward many theories of curriculum development evolved in an atmosphere of academic freedom.

In India, the curricula of universities and colleges, when these were set up by the British Government, followed the British pattern with a curriculum content approved by the British Government. Higher education, patterned during the colonial rule, in structure and content, did not change corresponding with the changes that came into the system of education in Britain later on. Consequently, the curricula of higher education in India remained a relic of Britain's colonial education, based on the traditional syllabi in the Arts and Sciences that prevailed in Britain in the early years of the twentieth century.[1]

# Curriculum Planning in Indian Universities

Indian universities followed, even after independence in 1947, the traditional method of inviting scholars from other colleges and universities as experts to select subject-matter content and present their recommendations at a meeting of a Board of Studies of a college or department of a university. The Board generally consisted of the Head of the college or the university department concerned, one or two elected members from the teaching staff, and invited experts.

Normally, curricular changes were suggested by the teachers, and the head of the department was expected to reflect their ideas at the meeting of the Board of Studies. But, in general, very few radical changes were suggested. Though there has been so far, to the knowledge of this author, no systematic study of the pace, quality, or the quantum of changes suggested by teachers in the curricula, it can be safely generalized from a cursory review of the records of Boards of Studies over time that university teachers functioned at a minimum necessary level of academic effort and were content to maintain the status quo in their academic spheres.

A number of experienced educators have attributed the apathetic attitude of teachers to not being involved from the beginning in planning the curriculum of their own departments in an atmosphere of freedom.* The Education Commission of 1966 commented:

> in many of the weaker colleges and universities a majority of teachers teach mechanically and listlessly.

---

* Refer listed Reading: Kulkarni

> The subjects in which they lecture do not often involve their intellectual passion. They do not usually have a part in the formulation of the syllabus which they are required to teach, nor do they make – with a few bright exceptions – experiments in methods of teaching.[2]

Both the administrative and academic hierarchical dominance of the heads and authorities of the Indian universities does not encourage a free and fearless exchange of views in academic matters. Also, the traditional attitude of reverence towards experienced older persons and seniors in office, and assumption of superiority in all matters on the part of senior academicians may not promote freedom of expression among the rank and file of the staff of the academic departments. This situation remains unchanged even at the end of the twentieth century in many academic institutions.

In the experience of the author, another noticeable feature of many of the universities of India, is a lack of intra-faculty communication of a professional or academic nature. When teachers get together in the course of their daily work, there is very little sharing of their work experience or discussion of common problems in their academic work. Teachers appear to feel highly inhibited to express their opinions and criticisms of the academic programme, of the scope for effective teaching, or the quality of evaluation and administrative actions taken in their institutions. This may be due to the perception of teachers that their future prospects of promotion depended a great deal on a congenial relationship with their seniors and administrators. Bringing about radical changes by the teachers in regard to the curriculum of a department of study is also dependent on the professional maturity, commitment, and scholarship, as well as an organizational climate of academic freedom.

Due to the lack of these above qualities in college teachers and institutions, even the prevailing infrastructure and opportunities are not fully exploited by teachers for improving the quality of higher education. It is necessary that teachers at every level have the professional competence, academic excellence and commitment to improve the quality of education within the present given infrastructure in the higher educational system. Developing such qualities should be the immediate task of teacher educators through appropriate curriculum planning for teacher education.

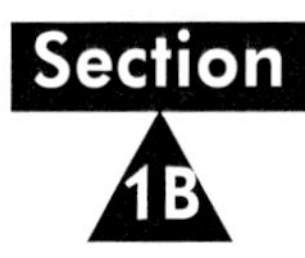


# The First Step in Curriculum Planning Developing a Philosophy of Education

Though the Government of India in 1984 called for a national debate on the educational policy framed by it, it did not touch upon the process of curriculum development followed in the universities and colleges of India. Many scholars of education have said that since the curriculum of an educational program is the tangible means of reaching the goals set by an educational system, curriculum planning is a crucial activity of academicians for which they need competency. Educators need to become familiar with some known approaches to curriculum development.

Though there may be many points of view over approaches to curriculum development, Tyler identified the first fundamental question as "What educational purposes should the school* seek to attend?"[3] Phenix, another eminent educationist, stated that preparing a curriculum was a problem in free societies because a choice must be made regarding the content, method, and order of instruction, so as to "...economize scarce learning potential by making a judicious and appropriate selection of study content," and that beliefs about what was best implied a scale of values, constituting the aims, objectives and purposes of education.[4]

Tyler observed that selecting objectives was a matter of choice and must be therefore considered as value judgements, which made a comprehensive philosophy of education a necessary guide for making these judgements.[5]

Discussing the importance of a philosophy of education, Brubacher, an outstanding educational philosopher, stated

* Refers to any educational institution

> Disavowal of philosophy as a basis for policy, implies action based on unexamined assumptions...
> A deliberate theory, a clearly thought out philosophy, enables one to guide the course of education by intelligence and foresight, rather than by hazard and happenstance.[6]

Similarly, India's eminent scholar and philosopher, Karan Singh, asserted:

> no nation can become great unless it has a coherent *dharma*, a fairly clear scale of values to which it is committed. In India this has now become confused and diluted. There has been tremendous economic growth, rapid expansion of education, highly developed science and technology in the last fifty-three years, but as a nation our moral fibre and intellectual calibre has declined, the responsibility for this lies squarely upon our educational system.[7]

Echoing the above opinion, Ghanchi stated "...the educational scenario conjures up an image of wastelands…" and the one reason was that "...we lack an honest clarity about the goals of higher education, and that is, philosophical clarity." Further, pointing 'out that one of three myths of higher education in India, was the `philosophical myth' that a sound philosophy of life underlay the Indian educational system. Ghanchi pointed out that the main burden of enquiry commissions was the glaring absence of a sound workable philosophy at the roots of our thinking on the policy for higher education and Curricula.[8]

Yet another scholar, Sundararajan, had this to say:

> Higher education in India has not responded to global or national needs, continues with an obsolete curriculum, without any suitable philosophy of education and no strategies for meeting the needs of youth. These were not of concern to the sporadic attempts at reform by the Education Commissions and hence education has drifted without any direction given by a national philosophy.[9]

Describing certain stresses and strains, that Ghanchi felt, 'squeezed' the Indian educational system, he mentioned one constraint as philosophical and stated that due to this the Indian higher education suffered from a psycho-moral-intellectual vacuum manifested in the meaninglessness of pursuit in the classrooms reflected in strikes etc.[10]

Even in the last decade of the twentieth century there has been very little noticeable effort made in universities toward formulating a statement of an educational philosophy for higher education as a basis for planning curricula in different disciplines.

A way of overcoming this lacuna in higher education has been indicated by the eminent educationist, Humayun Kabir, in a statement quoted below:

> Though we cannot point out to fully articulated and monolithic structure of thought as an Indian philosophy of education, we may, from the diverse discussions, on education by different sages and philosophers, build up a system of ideas which were inspired by the social ideals of ancient India.[11]

Not only in ancient India, but through all the later historical periods down to the twentieth century, there have been generations of saints, preceptors, scholars, social reformers, learned kings, scholarly administrators, and revolutionary leaders of social change who had shown, at one time or other, concern over the education of the young and offered their ideas on the philosophical foundations on which the education of people should be built.

Tyler stated that as a principle of curriculum development, a statement of the educational and social philosophy that an institution is committed to is the first screen through which the objectives of an educational program should be examined. If this is done, the selected objectives stand high in terms of values.[12] It is therefore possible and necessary that an explicit statement of a philosophy of education is attempted in the curriculum development effort in teacher education for teachers in colleges and universities.

# Developing a Philosophy of Education

The educational philosophy of a country has its roots in the life philosophies of the people of the country. Into the fabric of the common life philosophy of the people of India are woven the strands of many fine philosophies of the numerous religious and cultural movements that have gone into the making of a multi-faceted Indian society. Even though there may not be explicit statements of educational philosophy included in the philosophical statements underlying the various religious and cultural movements of the country, philosophical bases are implicit in the religious and cultural literature and practices of ancient, medieval and modern educational institutions, some of which have survived to the present age.

If a common, general, life philosophy of the Indian people is identified, it will be a major source of an educational philosophy that would include the common elements of the different educational philosophies prevailing in the country. If this is beyond reach, even if a consensus among national policy decision makers can be achieved for a national educational philosophy, it can be expected to. lead to an educational system relevant to the socio-cultural realities of India. Otherwise it will be difficult to formulate an overall national philosophy of education that is so important to build a cohesive nation (Appendix 1).

However, Brubacher pointed out that the basis of educational philosophy is not dependent solely on life philosophies but also on data drawn from various other sources. He said that the process of developing educational philosophy starts with

> the 'humble data of common sense' and gathers into this bag, data from science and history, paying special attention to life sciences of biology and psychology, and social sciences of sociology, politics and economics, as well as educational history. The data of morals and religion too should be added.[13]

To search for consensus among competing philosophies of education, it is best to start with the "concrete field of educational practice rather than the abstract field of educational theory, the area of educational tactics rather than that of educational strategy", says Brubacher, stressing that a consensus is necessary for a society to be cohesive.[14a] Statements on areas of agreement in educational practices and educational philosophy, as a basis for consensus, identified from the discussions by Brubacher and Tyler are presented below. These illustrate the concrete field of educational practice and the area of educational tactics as a starting point to search for a consensus.

## 2.1 Areas of Agreement in Educational Practices and Educational Philosophies*

1. ***Obvious matters*** such as making school buildings safe against fire hazards, protecting children against traffic hazards, providing glasses to wear for children who need them etc., and compulsory attendance up to a minimum level. Making compulsory vaccination of children before attending school is another consensus area. Also that only teachers who can meet certification requirements should be allowed to teach.

2. ***Proximate aims of education***: Command of fundamental processes of communication and computation, health, competency in family, civic, and vocational relations; worthy use of leisure: and ethical sensitivity.

   A sizable portion of the race experiences should be the common heritage of all; and the three 'Rs' at the lower level

* The statements are based on the discussions in the following books
a) *Modern Philosophies of Education*, *Op.cit.*, pp. 351–357
b) *Basic Principles of Curriculum and Instruction*, *Op.cit.*, pp. 22–24.

and the trivium – grammar, logic, and rhetoric at the upper levels, are indispensable to all.

3. ***Basic Knowledge*** of history, social and physical sciences, and inclusion of some of the sharper issues, which divide the body politics.

4. ***The several methods of instruction*** – their selection and use depending on circumstances; drill at the proper time and place; an important place for the problem method; and universally accepted answers in arithmetic, grammar, or health which may be indoctrinated

5. ***Freedom for the individual to arrive at his solution*** – Freedom as a method, and freedom as an end of the educative process.

6. ***Need for motivating instruction,*** as children learn better if interested, and if the curriculum arises out of children's/ students' present experiences.

7. ***Individuality*** to be cultivated but not a cult of individualism.

8. ***That there is a science of education*** by which variables can be studied and the consequences of certain educational practices can be determined. Scientific techniques like intelligence testing can be put to use in instruction in certain fields of education.

9. ***Democratic practices*** are shown in planning the curriculum, in practical problems of classroom management, and sharing with students in decision-making.

10. ***The Curriculum***: The school should conserve the social heritage of race experience, and consequently, exercise a normative as well as a conservative function in selecting the curriculum.

There is agreement on the following:

1. When the natural order in life is accepted, the proximate aims of education deals with an analysis of life and culture

here and now, and motivation depends on an understanding of the basic drives of human nature.

2. There are two principal theories of the ways of knowing, or the theory of knowledge: one the morphological, or trying to get at the essential form of material undergoing learning, and the other – the experimental, concerned with successfully adapting means to ends in the solution of some problems which is obstructing action. These are not mutually exclusive. The resulting knowledge is held to be tentatively true.

3. Knowledge as its own end has a spiritual value, and hence both naturalists and supernaturalists will agree on this ultimate aim of education.

4. The principal object of value in the whole educational programme is the pupil himself, that is, the dignity of the individual and the respect for human personality. Democratic philosophies of education identify themselves with this concept.

5. Democratic philosophies of education favour a pluralistic theory of state, in which the state is only one of the social agencies of education, providing the individual a choice of schools to attend. In a pluralistic state both private and public schools will be approved for the same reason.

Similar to the philosophic positions described above are the following statements by Tyler:

> Every human being is important, regardless of race or national, social and economic status. Opportunity should be found for wider participation in all social activities in the social groups of the society. Variability, rather than a single type of personality, should he encouraged. Faith should be placed in intelligence as the method for dealing with important problems, rather than faith in the authority of an autocratic *or* an aristocratic group. In essence, the statement of philosophy attempts to define the nature of a good life and a good society.

Summarising briefly the content of educational philosophy expounded above so far, it can be stated as below:

> the pluralistic positive approach is one that is appropriate to democracies, and it involves the family and religious institutions too as educational agencies. In a democracy, there is value for the dignity of man, egalitarianism, freedom and sharing.
>
> An economic system, with a few having wealth and leisure, may encourage the attitude of indifference towards menial labor and the less privileged classes of society. But a democratic system may encourage the attitude that no labor or work is degrading, and that all work is inherently dignified. This outlook insists on claiming a larger and more just portion of the surplus of wealth and leisure of the economic system, for the benefit of the working class.

Brubacher argued that philosophic agreements too are possible and therefore consensus among educational philosophers is possible, provided there is adequate communication between different philosophers and an effort is made apply a scientific approach to resolving differences.[14b]

# Section 3 Sources of Educational Philosophy in India

There are not many publications of texts that present the philosophical viewpoints on education in the philosophical literature of India. Few are the attempts made to present a systematic analysis, classification, and synthesis of the philosophical foundations of education in India. The lack of a philosophic approach in higher education, and "superimposition, outwardly of western outlook on life has led to a philosophical schizophrenia," said Ghanchi, deploring that "students and teachers do not have an exact philosophical goal to approximate through their intellectual exercises," and tracing the 'psycho-moral intellectual vacuum' to philosophical constraints.[15]

In developing a philosophy of teacher education in India, as Kabir advised, it may be relevant to seek the basis in the philosophies of life evolved in India. Philosophical views on education, though implicit, are available beginning with the oral vedic literature up to the fifth century B.C. and from classical Sanskrit and Tamil literature in the early historical period. Philosophical literature is abundant in many regional languages of India, spanning the period roughly from about the 5th century B.C. to about the eighteenth century A.D. and even onwards to the present days. Much of the philosophic lore is present in the form of lyrics, epics, ballads and poems, and dramas of this period, and in traditional oral forms too.

There are scholarly works on polity, economics, ethics, logic, health, healing, family life and maternity, home management, culinary arts, fine arts, architecture, and agriculture and tamed animal life, during the early centuries of India's history, in which are embedded religious and social philosophies of the people of India. The discourses of great saints and teachers who founded many schools of religion and philosophy in Hinduism, Buddhism and Jainism of India, the teachings of missionaries of Christianity, Islam and Hebrewism and Zoroastrianism of the Arabian lands, Confucianism and Taoism of the Orient, have all given rise to many life philosophies among the people of India.

These have influenced the philosophical aspects of education in great many indigenous semi-religious schools found all over rural and urban areas of India. There is also the influence of a sizeable population of the tribal people's philosophical beliefs about life and nature on the popular beliefs and cultural practices of the people of India. There is therefore a rich source of life philosophies from which elements that would form a foundation for national indigenous educational philosophy can be identified.

Explicit philosophical statements leading to state level educational policies emerged on the Indian scene only after the British rule was established sometime in the early nineteenth century. Current educational practices, in general, do not lend themselves to a neat classification into one or the other known schools of philosophy. Some systems of educational practices in India can be identified somewhat as predominantly reflecting one or the other religious or social philosophy as in the case of Christian Mission Schools, Ramakrishna Mission schools, Santiniketan, the Rishi valley school, Arya Samaj schools, the Karve University for women, the Benaras Hindu University, the Aligarh Muslim University, Wardha schools of basic education, Gujarat Vidyapeeth, and such others.

Any attempt at formulating an overall statement of an Indian philosophy of education needs to be based on a study of all the religious, philosophical, humanistic, sociological, psychological, and scientific literature in publications. At present there are a very few publications which set forth discussions on what the Indian philosophy of education is or should be, though there are many newspaper and journal articles on this theme. There are very few textbooks that, on the basis of a systematic analysis and classification have consolidated the philosophical views on education expressed by generations of philosophers, scholars, and reformists, who have dominated the socio-religious history of India. However, as an introduction to an Indian philosophy of education, a comprehensive and compact review of the philosophies of India from the vedic ages to the twentieth century, with an independent statement of the fundamentals of an Indian philosophy of education, is available in an easily readable form in the book: *Indian Philosophy of Education* by Humayun Kabir, especially in the section titled "Indian Philosophy of Education".[16]

A detailed discussion of the sources of Indian philosophic literature with its historical background is given in the following pages for enrichment of one's understanding of the roots of life philosophies of India. The reader may skip the following part of this section if not interested in this aspect and proceed to the next section, without loss of continuity in the text.

## 3.1 Indian Sources of Philosophic Literature and Implications for the Educational Philosophies of India

One approach to identifying India's educational philosophy may be to apply the same four questions that Brubacher asked for identifying the western philosophies of life that gave rise to their educational philosophies.

In response to the first question: "What is the nature of Reality?" one gathers from the Upanishads* that the Creator first created Energy and Matter for interacting to produce all forms of existence, the active and the inert. Further, for all life there is an external world of senses and an inner self—the gross and the subtle, the latter, born out of 'jivatman' or self, which is part of the universal self or *Paramatman*.

While the external world, which includes the body, decays, the 'self' that merges with the Brahman—the Universal spirit,

* The Upanishads contain the philosophic portions of the Vedas.

endures. Those who understand this self know Reality. In the Ishopanishad it is said "in the heart of all things, whatever there is in the universe, dwells the Lord. He alone is Reality." Therefore, seeking an understanding of the self in relation to all its manifestations and to the universal self is the highest goal of education. A subsequent goal to this is the cultivation of reverence for all life.

From the Vedas emerge the message of unity in the diversity and multiplicity of the forms by which one Supreme Being is known, couched in the following words: 'Truth is one: sages call it by various names.'

In general, almost all the schools of philosophy comprising 'Hinduism' consider Creation as existing at two levels: the material and the spiritual, the spiritual being pervasive over all creation. This concept underlies also the religious philosophies of Buddhism, Jainism, and Sikhism, and is reflected in all the preaching and discourses of saints and acharyas of all these religions of India over the past centuries up to the present. Differences in the schools of philosophy in all these religions of India lie in the interpretations of the way the material and the spiritual aspects related to each other, chiefly, if dualistic in nature or monistic.

As to the second question: "What is the nature of existence? Are Change, Novelty, and Time, the generic traits of existence, or are they only appearances? Hinduism, Buddhism, Jainism, and Sikhism believe in the idea of a cyclic existence linked to an eternal existence, timeless and endless. Accordingly, human life in the world is caught in a cycle of births and deaths, caused by lapses in righteous conduct, in one span of existence or 'janma'. Only by improving on one's righteous conduct, as prescribed in religious scriptures and preachings of holy persons, can one's existence become gradually free of lapses until one escapes the cycle of "Karma' to merge with the universal and eternal spirit.

The nature of human existence, which is full of seemingly unaccountable and unjustifiable events, is given an explanation by the theory of Karma. A positive approach to facing life is implied, as the possibility of changing one's destiny is entertained. The theory of Karma creates a frame of mind that puts up with what is seen as unjust or underserved. No school of Indian philosophy accepted evil as the ultimate reality, but promoted hope of an improved future if effort was toward a better self in the present.[17]

The Buddha gave more importance to life seen and experienced, as the reality, needing to be managed for the welfare of mankind through the moderate path of conduct, and a charitable attitude towards less fortunate beings in the community. Kabir observed that the most significant feature of the ancient Indian outlook on life was its comprehensiveness.[18]

Human condition is described in the Upanishads in the following ways:

> Each one of us is a center of life, a unique event in the universe, and whatever our external relations to people and things may be, the absolute fact remains that we have to live our inner life alone even as we have to die our own death. No one can live our inner life for us; no one can go through our own death.[19]

In general, the above beliefs as to the nature of reality and the nature of existence found expression in recognizing all life as sacred and a part of a supreme universal self, compassion as a noble quality of human nature, faith in a supreme sprit, and humility as necessary to gain true knowledge and vision.

Education accordingly should give importance to doing one's duties devotedly, a positive approach to life and improving constantly upon one's rightful conduct.

The third question to be asked is: What is the nature of human nature? In the view of India's religions, human nature is pulled between bodily desires and the mind that is aware of the harm done to the health of a person by uncontrolled indulgence.[20] All schools of Indian philosophy recognize man's many-sided nature. According to the Samkhya school, human personality has three elements: 1) the soul, 2) the subtle body of the senses and the mind, the intellect the motor organs, and 3) the gross body which is the visible body composed of material elements. Similarly, the Upanishads envisioned five sheaths, from the subtle to the gross, as covering the self.[21]

Education, according to Samkhya Yoga, "is the means to develop the physical and the subtle body so that the soul or spirit can express itself unhampered by any of the limitations imposed by them". In the Upanishads, "the object of education is to train and exercise the five koshas..." to make them fit instruments for the good life," characterized by a spirit of action and enjoyment free from all attachment.[22]

Human nature is perceived to be weak but amenable to being strengthened through rigorous yogic exercises, faith in the power of the mind over the body, and an abstemious life-style.[23] From the Upanishads we get the message that what one practices one becomes, implying that the means are as important as the ends. A great proponent of this principle in the twentieth century was Mahatma Gandhi who exemplified this philosophic principle through his life and writings.[24]

Religious scriptures of India also stress that a human being needs the help of an enlightened teacher to reach mental and spiritual heights. Generally man is not strong enough in mind and spirit to singly strive for spiritual emancipation, and therefore the teacher is to be revered and emulated. This view of human nature is reflected in the development of the 'gurukul' system of education and the tradition of seeking out a worthy teacher. The gurukuls applied the belief that human nature changed through practising what the sacred scriptures set forth as good conduct, rather than by accumulating factual knowledge of what the great men and women and the holy scriptures prescribed.[25]

A material view of the universe, seems to he the general view of modern man, ruled by modern mechanism based on scientific materialism.[26] This material view of the universe 'reduces all to matter, or electrons, or energy, and our brain to a machine,' 'reduces consciousness to an energy merely emanating from the brain,' and which reduces the universe to a universe of quantity and intellectual abstractions wherein the end of all things are dust and fall into dust and death.[27] But, besides this view, we have a universe of spiritual radiance from which this universe of matter is only a reflection, a world of Spirit..., the universe of eternal beauty which has been felt by all the greatest seers and poets and spiritual men of all times, where all things are in life and go into life.[28]

Three attitudes of mind and three types of knowledge, that a human being is capable of, are referred to in the following statements:

> All things on earth, from a flower to a human being, can be an object of love or contemplation, an object of intellectual interest, and an object of possession. In the first case they give the freedom of joy in the infinite; in the second they give us that knowledge which is power; in the third they give us the chain that binds us to matter, drag us down to the darkness of death, to the miseries of competition for selfish power, instead of cooperation for unselfish joy.[29]

"Those three attitudes of mind, those three types of knowledge, are well described in the Bhagavad Gita," says Mascaros, quoting verse XVII, 20–22.

The Upanishads, the Gita, and later philosophical teachings stressed the value of love and wisdom over the value of formal scholarship; stressed on the value of doing one's duty without expecting a reward, of unquestioning belief in the grace of God, shown by devotion to God in any form, and of rejecting worldly pleasure.

These philosophical views were layered over with Jainism's stress on extreme compassion for all life, each lifetime considered as a phase in a chain of cause and effect, in which effort for better future should be made. Three ways and five vows of conduct prescribed in Jainism were:

> Right faith, not blind acceptance but reasoned; right knowledge, knowing the real nature of ego and non-ego,

> and freedom from doubt, error, and uncertainty; right conduct; seeking truth, not spreading untruth, renouncing worldly attachments, showing kindness in speech and action. not killing, self-discipline, not stealing, and devotion to God.[30]

The Buddha who was pragmatic, preached compassion and concern with making life, here and now, happy in the mortal world. He placed value on all life, on seeking truth, renouncing worldly attachments, and showing kindness in speech and action. The basic tenets of Buddha included the doctrine of the Middle Path: non-violence, non-hatred, friendliness to all, renunciation, continence, and the ideal of reaching nirvana.[31]

Most of his tenets came to be accepted by large sections of Hindus and assimilated in Hinduism, and the Buddha came to be regarded as an avatar.

Besides religious instruction, Buddhist centers of learning also taught medicine, agriculture, dairy farming, logic, grammar, architecture, and art. Jainism and Buddhism emerged with many other heterodox creeds in the period of 800 B.C.–500 B.C. The Hindu revival that followed was influenced by Buddhist methods of organising learning centers as was seen in the Sankara Mutts' and other similar centers established by Sankara and many Vaishnavait 'acharyas' in later years.[32]

From the ancient days there were also the life philosophies of non-vedic religious systems followed by such as the Natha, Yoga, Siddhacara cults. Other early sources of life philosophies are epics like the Ramayana and Mahabharata, and 'puranas' like the Vishnu purana and the Bhagavatham. These have been the sources of philosophical guidance as well as moral code of conduct for many generations of Indians. All these different religious movements and religious works brought in a great deal of diversity in the life philosophies of the people and since these were theosophical, intellectual and spiritual discourses and movements without the element of coercion, a spirit of tolerance pervaded the Indian society even in the days of British rule.[33]

After the tenth century, with the entry of Islamic rule in India, a distinct stream of educational philosophy, educational practices and educational system spread its influence and existed side by side with all other educational systems already prevailing in India. But with the break-up of the Mughal empire in the eighteenth century A.D., a period of political instability followed, during which time all the indigenous systems of education in India stagnated, surviving only on local patronage, and continuing in set traditional patterns.

## 3.2 The Age of the Mystics

During the troubled period of India's history from the thirteenth to the eighteenth century, in the face of periodic religious oppression of a few rulers, internal strife among the declining Indian kingdoms, and the impoverishment of the rural countryside under an oppres-sive feudatory system of landlordism and subservient peasantry, there appeared a string of mystics, seers, and saintly poets, belonging to different sects, castes, and religions.

They bridged all religions in their preachings, affirmed faith in the might of the Supreme Force to overcome evil, and became popular leaders of the poor and the oppressed. They gave spiritual and moral education to the people though it was informal and unorganized. These spiritual leaders represented the second wave of the 'bhakti' movement who spread an all-encompassing philosophy of life that gave solace to the common people. Their lives served as models for the masses. Their devotional songs contained a liberal philosophy of life that fortified the moral and spiritual life and encouraged the coexistence of people of different faiths.[34]

## 3.3 Later Immigrant Religions as Sources of Educational Philosophies in India

In the early eighth century A.D. many Zoarastrians fleeing from religious persecution in Persia by invading Islamic forces, sought refuge as traders on the west coast of India and added their life philosophies to the existing social and religious streams of philosophies in India. They became known as Parsees who lived in harmony with other communities and by their industry, integrity and intelligence, contributed a great deal to the prosperity of India through their leadership in many walks of life. The motto of the religion was 'Good thoughts, good words and good deeds'. It was firmly believed that good will ultimately overcome evil. Zarathyushtra, the founder of the religion, insisted on the equality of the sexes, and freedom of choice to a child at initiation into the religion, and advised silent meditation. He stressed purity in thought, word and deed. Value for the welfare of human and animal life and for truth and uprightness in action were reflected in the Parsees' philosophy of education, and the Parsees built many charitable institutions and educational institutions by making generous financial endowments.[35]

With regard to the impact of the religious philosophy of Islam "it did not lead to any marked change in the educational thought and practices"that prevailed in the country, but there was a change from the religious bias to the secular bias in that equal opportunities for education was given to members of all communities, importance was given to the practical arts and to directing education to follow a child's interests and understanding rather than to the traditional method of learning the alphabet and reciting from books.[36] Islam preached brotherhood, concern for the poor, and value for truth, humility, honesty, chastity, and justice.[37] "Prophet Mohammad also emphasized in the Hadith the need to resist injustice, discrimination and inequality." Islam prohibits 'unbridled usury; gambling, prostitution, and alcohol consumption, and advocates the distribution of the wealth of the community to all members according to their needs.[37]

The Ten Commandments of Christianity stressed more or less the same values, and gave importance to the power of love over brute force. Jesus Christ through parables and exemplary acts of compassion spread the message of love, sacrifice, and the spirit of service to mankind: Between the fifteenth and eighteenth centuries Christian missionaries brought about a more organized form of education through their mission schools which were open to all citizens, in which they applied western philosophies of education of Europe and England. The western philosophy of education was imbibed gradually also by the educated class and became implicit in the philosophy of education reflected in the various reform movements during the British rule.[38]

In the fifteenth century, a disciple of Kabir, Guru Nanak, founded Sikhism synthesizing the core values of Hinduism and Islam. Arjun, the fifth guru, established the Adi Granth, the holy scripture of the Sikhs, in which both the religious rituals and worship of idols of the Hindus, as well as the religious observances and worship at Mecca of the Muslims were rejected. Sikhism did not recognize caste or creed distinctions, stood for freedom and equality for women with men. Purity of life, loyalty, chastity, honesty, justice, mercy and temperance were the virtues on which vital stress was laid.[39] The Jews too found a place of refuge in India but it is doubtful if the Jewish religious philosophy influenced the people, but there was no hostility towards the Jews due to the existence of religious tolerance in the country.

A more detailed narrative of the history of the several religious and philosophical schools is given in an appendix* but it is sufficient to note here that though there was wide variation in the religions of India, mass religious persecution by rulers or powerful sects have not been common, and with a few exceptions in the history of religious development in India a spirit of tolerance dominated. A study of the life philosophies of the different religions of India shows that they influenced one another so that a common core of a philosophy of life can be identified. It should not be therefore difficult to develop a common philosophical basis for educational programs acceptable to different cultural groups of any region in India.

Moreover, as mentioned earlier, there are other sources for developing a philosophy of education such as biological sciences,

---

* Appendix II, Historical Sources of Life Philosophies of India.

records of human experience in history, sociology, politics, economics and psychology, as well as aesthetic arts and literature. The data from these fields contribute to shared understanding of views of life, nature and human development among the educated people so that the development of an overall philosophy of education is possible. Whatever educational philosophy has guided the educational system in India so far can be said to be implicit in the state educational policies that were framed from the time of the establishment of the British rule in the early nineteenth century, and state patronage in 1835 with the acceptance of McCauley's Minutes on education. Likewise, educational philosophy underlying the educational system of independent India is implicit in the reports of education commissions of the Government of India.

Section 4

# Philosophical Guidelines for a Curriculum in Teacher Education of College Teachers

Life philosophies of India as a source of educational philosophies can be studied from a number of texts published, some of which are listed under ' Readings' at the end of section three on sources of Educational Philosophy in India. Another source is a study by this author endeavoring to identify, ideas on educational philosophies, in general and in particular on teacher education, expressed by Indian educators and scholars. For this purpose, statements reflecting educational philosophy and ideas on different aspects of education were collected from books, articles and research studies on education published in India

These statements were grouped and classified under different aspects of education to which they were relevant. The statements were collected from all the articles on higher education and teacher education published in reports, journals and newspapers between 1990 and 2003, a span of thirteen years*. The statements were classified under thirteen aspects of education that were identified, and those that focused on educational philosophy for higher education were selected as a source for developing the philosophy of teacher 'education, In addition, statements of value-preferences in six areas of professional competency of college teachers identified in a research study by the same author can form another source of educational philosophy for teacher education.**

---

* Appendix III.

** P.S. Chari, "Identifying Standards of Excellence for Professional Education of College Teachers," *Journal of Educational Planning and Administration* (Vol.XIV:8), New Delhi: National Institute of Educational Planning and Administration.

Even if all these sources are available, formulating a composite statement of educational philosophy for teacher education is an arduous task for teacher educators. Fortunately, there are a few textbooks on philosophy of education that may offer a starting base. Using these above sources an attempt at defining educational philosophy for teacher educations is made, starting with the points of view that arise from a few general major issues pertaining to teacher education in India. The positions taken in regard to these points of view in the issues, within the framework of broader philosophical guidelines, will help to define the philosophical stand to be taken for teacher education.

## 4.1 Major Issues Relevant to Teacher Education*

Should teacher education spearhead changes in the educational system by

a) taking up a participatory role in planning and administration of higher education?

b) preparing educators who would be critical of the status quo in education and society and be pro-active, and further, develop the ability to be innovative in planning and leaching aimed at social progress, or, should teacher education uphold the status quo in society and prepare teachers who resign themselves to the prevailing conditions and accept a passive role in the educational system?

Should teacher education focus on the total personality development of teachers or only on professional competence in transmitting of information?

Should teacher education in institutions act only as a source of manpower to meet the demands for teachers as and when necessary, or aim at teacher education as a lifelong process for continuously improving teaching standards, research and conditions favourable to high quality teaching?

---

* Major issues listed above include suggestions from *Criteria for Curriculum Decisions in Teacher Education*, Washington D.C: Assocn for Supervision and Curriculum Development, 1963.

Should teacher education give priority to treating teaching as a profession with a mission and as a social: service, or to treating teaching as a job for earning a livelihood?

In these and many other issues what stand should be taken will have to reckon with the prevailing socio-economic contexts and the changes that are taking place. The following statements reflecting the educational philosophy made by Indian educators and scholars in relation to their stand on these major issues offer a framework of philosophical guidelines for developing a curriculum for teacher education of college teachers. Those that have a special implication for teacher education of home science teachers are noted.

Since the statements are on different aspects of education expressed by various educators and scholars, some may be broad generalizations and some specific and concrete, and some having ideas clubbed together covering different aspects of education. This compilation, it should be emphasized, offers only a framework of reference in developing the curriculum of teacher education, as already stated above.

There are thirteen areas of reference in the framework under which educational philosophy statements have been grouped, giving some structure for definition of a philosophic basis for developing a curriculum for teacher education of college teachers by teacher educators. Only statements reflecting educational philosophy have been picked out of several statements on aspects of the educational system, are presented below. A full list of statements offering a framework of reference for developing a curriculum for teacher education, compiled from literature, textbooks and research studies, is given in appendix IV.

## 4.2 Defining Statements of Educational Philosophy for Teacher Education in General[40]*

1. It is important to have a national philosophy for education and the educational system to prevent educational drift and unorganized expansion.

2. "There should be a holistic approach in educational policies, stressing convergence, not conflict, and cooperation but not unhealthy competition.

3. There should be holistic approach in teacher education leading to development of the total personality of the teacher, and the personality development of teachers should be considered as important as their professional competence, because teaching can be done even by being its role model.*

4. In higher education we need radical and broad humanism, dynamic secularism, and a synthesis of material and spiritual values. Holistic approach is reflected in what is termed as humanistic approach to education (Clement, 1993, The Hindu). The humanistic approach presupposes"... a reverence for the kaleidoscopic mystery of human life and experience," "seeks to release us from the bondage of the tyranny of custom and deification of untested orthodoxies," implies "opportunity to become human...." Creativity, idealism and concern for environment define humanism (Max, U.News, March 21, 1994). Education should stand for tolerance, and intolerance of intolerance, and compassion as part of Indian ethics.

5. Education is an acculturating force and also a liberating and empowering one, if operating in a cultural environment of freedom.

6. Education cannot be totally value free as it involves value choices in promoting spiritual, ethical, and cultural values. It is value orientation of every learner, not just transmission of information, but also of certain ethical, moral, and personal academic values, for gaining wisdom in using knowledge in own and mankind's interest. Values determine human nature more than the amount of information. Wisdom is gained when knowledge is purified on values.*

7. There is danger to society in placing faith in expertise alone without an integrated wholesome view of life.

8. Purism in education that is not in touch with realities causes acute crisis of relevance in the education of people. Education draws its data and inspiration from daily existence. Eclecticism should be adopted in the approach to higher education.

9. Education should be perceived as having multifarious roles: social, cultural. economic, technological and political. Education has a humanizing role by harmonizing technology and moral and higher traditional values.

10. Education should show a proactive role in a changing society, in conformity to educational and social realities that are changing technology and resources constraints, and be responsive to problems of industry, commerce and other social activities.

    The goals of teacher education should therefore go beyond preparing teachers for fulfilling the immediate aims of particular educational institutions, to include the long-term goals of education and involvement of educators in social issues. Therefore, education for social responsibilities should be included in the education for the teaching profession.*

11. Education should aim at divinity, dignity and excellence, pursuit of knowledge and truth, developing commitment to academic excellence, and of altruistic qualities. Especially, education of teachers should instil the attitude that those who seek knowledge and truth should not seek wealth and power at the cost of pursuit of knowledge and truth.

12. Education should stand for progress, adventure of ideas, pushing the frontiers of knowledge, for reason, for removal of ignorance, superstition, bigotry and removal of intolerance.*

13. Education should stand for creation of a scientific temper as seen in search for truth, advancement of frontiers of learning, by cultivating curiosity, ability to think and spirit of enquiry.

14. Education should promote faith in the idea of liberty, equality and fraternity, faith in justice that transcends sectarian beliefs and reflects democratic values.

15. Education should stand for improving the quality of life of the common man, ensuring a minimum level of quality of life by providing highest education for at least a few, and basic education for all.
16. Equality of opportunity for higher education should be provided but should not be equated with quality of achievement, which should be the criterion for right to higher education playing the role in creating an equitable society.
17. Education should be looked upon as a lifelong process, its purpose being to move from the level of information through a cultural level to an emancipated level to self-realisation. The educative process should be looked upon as a continuous, evolving, changing and growing discipline, requiring teachers to be in touch with developments in the subject of education.
18. In planning a teacher education curriculum, faith in democratic procedures should be promoted by involving student-teachers, teacher-educators, educational administrators, educational psychologists, sociologists and eminent citizens in the planning process.
19. The formal educational system should be thought of as a component of a larger. comprehensive educational system of the total society, consisting of informal educational agencies such as the audio-visual mass media, exhibitions, libraries, journals, newspapers and markets.
20. Teacher Education should give importance to the teacher's role of improving professional input by drawing upon the teaching experience of teacher educators and their perceptions of the realities of the professional and social contexts in which teaching needs to be done.
21. In the teacher education programs, the prospective teacher should be looked upon as a part of a faculty who should fit harmoniously into the social milieu of a professional group, the student group, the administrative setup and the alumni (Cronkite, 1950, p.158 ).

22. Teacher education institutions should look upon student teachers as cooperating researchers capable of systematic study of the daily teaching-learning processes and improving the educational system. For this, a spirit of enquiry should permeate the teacher education programmes, which may be expected to carry over to the professional life of the prospective teachers.
23. Teacher education programmes should prepare teachers who can play multiple roles such as a guide and moral support in a context of social change, a mediating role among various social groups, acting on rational grounds when conflicting social forces may be at play, and a participatory role at the level of university decision-making.*
24. The education of teachers should promote the attitude that teaching is a most important profession for a society, and help them to identify themselves with great teachers so that they will be inspired to strive for great heights in their professional career.
25. Teacher education should promote a scientific attitude towards teaching, recognizing teaching as a complex task with a scientific basis.
26. Teacher education should be based on the belief that there are no permanent categories of good and bad teachers but performance depends on situations and times. There should be belief that everyone can attain excellence in something by striving for excellence
27. Structures within the educational system should be both indigenous and modern. Western models and any foreign models of an educational system should not be imitated thoughtlessly.
28. Teaching should be considered as work of an interdisciplinary nature, and hence development of a broad spectrum of abilities is an important goal. Hence teacher education curriculum, especially that of college home science

teachers, should he a blend of liberal education and specialization in the field of education, since home science is multidisciplinary in content.*

29. The educational system of India should not impose a homogenous curriculum on a heterogeneous society, neglecting individual differences and backgrounds, important as educational philosophy for home science teachers.*

30. The control of education should not be in the hands of any single external group. (a) Academic personnel should play a significant role in determining the curriculum, as they are the people who create knowledge. (b) (a. Uberoi 1988, A. of Higher Education; b. Chalam,2003, U. News).

The philosophical guidelines presented above can be expanded as more and more insights into the teaching and learning processes and into the nature of subject fields are gained by teacher educators. The next stage in the development of the teacher education curriculum is the identification of the goals of teacher education programmes in general and with reference to preparing home science teachers. In the following chapter in line with the guidelines presented above, certain broad goals of teacher education are discussed. This section on the philosophy of teacher education is mainly intended to stir interest in teacher educators to think about the philosophy of education they would want to apply in developing a curriculum for teacher education programs for which they are responsible.

Every school of educational philosophy may show some conceptual limitations and anachronisms in the context of expanding scientific knowledge of the world and of life in it. It will be wise to recognize that very few people can postulate a comprehensive finalized philosophy of education that is adequate for a lifetime. It is expected that a teacher's educational philosophy will change in course: of time with experience in the subject field, expansion of professional knowledge and increase in the total of knowledge of human psychology and sociology.

❖ ❖ ❖

# Reference Notes

**Reference Notes:** Ghanchi, *Op.cit.*, p. 1–7.

"It is axiomatic that academic freedom is one of the most to impact wielding ingredients that determine the quality of educators in a given environment "(p.5)

"This is why as an ideal to inform the thinking and practice of education, academic freedom has been coveted intensely, fought for valiantly, and guarded jealously all these years the world over,"

"Unfortunately the academic world in India too has not been free from the spinal weakness of abjuring the right to be free in thought and action,"

"Obviously, higher education in India to be a world class education would require an environment of freedom, innovation, experimentation and enterprise" (p.6)

"It is such hazardous recourse to a divergent way in respect of Indian higher education that could have changed the educational scenario of the country,"

"Regrettably, therefore both in concept and practice our education has continued to remain stuck in the same didactic, prescriptive, reactive, traditional rut the British had bequeathed us when they left the Indian shores," (p.7).

From "Education and Traditional Values: a Symposium," *The Education Quarterly*, Vol.XV, No.50 (June, 1963)

Concern of education is with specifically human values that are absolute eternal Values.

Educational process is to provide growth of this inherent sense of values.

Education is not shaping of educand to a set pattern, but awakening into growth of specific human element in the individuals, not indoctrination.

Education is helping individuals to experience some objective values contained in the 'goods of culture' and get committed to realize them.

Education should help distinguish between tradition that helps and tradition that hampers. The role of absolute values embedded in tradition is not to ensure fossilized perpetuation of the past.

—*Zakir Hussain*

Some traditional values have come down through the centuries in 'broken and partial forms', lingering as customs or habits, which cannot be integrated with the modern educational system.

The traditional values that are valid at present are

1. belief in one omnipotent Brahman of which many are the parts;
2. attitudes of 'intolerant – tolerance' or 'tolerance – intolerance' due to exigencies of history through adjustment and absorption of roles, forceful occupation and immigrant settling.;
3. compassion and understanding, constantly preached by medieval poet-saints, in the face of the miseries of prolonged feudal oppression, caste cruelties, and religious quarrels.

Changes in the concept of education are:

1. old transcendentalism has given away to the liberal and socialist European theory of the possibility of the achievement of the happiness of the greatest number as the summum bonum, with a shift from individual salvation to general human happiness.
2. The new education system places man in the center, has to build securely on new formulations about the psychology of modern man, aim at releasing kinetic and creative faculties of children, technological education, adult education and adjustment to contemporary needs and interests created by the input of inventive sciences.
3. The educational system should help the transformation of a feudal society into a modern society, by avoiding revival of outmoded moral values, imitative acceptance of everything from the west, and attempt a synthesis of the most genuine operative values of the past and the really vital values of a dynamic Europe, holding science for enquiry and music for harmony. *—Mulk Raj Anand*

Shifting of creative urges industrialization and mass production leading to escapism from the stresses and tension of the present through disproportionate pre-occupation with the future and an attraction to everything new, with little concern for proper values are to be deplored. Tolerance and charity should be an essential experience in the task of seeking and finding truth.

Holding genuine respect for the human being as the base of harmony, faith in the intrinsic good in humanity as the foundation of co-existence, and reconciling heritage with technology as the need of the hour. *— Kamala Devi Chattopadyaya*

Humanism: There are three forms of humanism. One, theocratic form emphasizes life's spiritual oneness, acts of righteousness, love, and compassion and spreading these moral aspects.

Another form, the anthropometric humanism, chiefly pursued by biologists and medical men, is concerned with human beings rather than all life on earth, the well being of the individual and of the species.

A third form of humanism is known as biometric humanism, sees life as a unified whole and exhorts man to ensure the well-being and survival of all life. All these concepts do not conflict with one another but form important components of the holistic approach to education.

E.Max. Extracts from "Humanism, Education and Development: The University – Community link," *University News* March 21, 1994.

## References Cited

[1] Ganchi, D.A. "Academic Freedom: The Fractious Scenario of Indian Higher Education," *University News* (September 23, 1966), pp. 5–7 and 11.

[2] Government of India, Report of Education Commission, 1966, *Op.cit.*, p. 278.

[3] Tyler, R.W., *Basic Principles of Curriculum and Instruction: Syllabus for Education 305.* Chicago: University Press, University of Chicago, pp.1, 2.

[4] Phenix, P., "The Nature of Curriculum," *School and Society* (eds ) Gross, C.H., Wronsky, S.P., and T.W. Hanson, Boston: D.L.Heath and Company,1962. pp. 394, 395.

[5] Tyler, R.W. *Op.cit.*, p. 3.

[6] Brubacher, J., *Bases for Policy in Higher Education*. New York: McGraw Hill Book Company, 1965. pp. 1–5.

[7] Singh, Karan. Foreword to the *Indian Theory of Education*, by N.A.Bourai, Delhi: Publishing Corporation, 1993.

[8] Ghanchi, B., "Three Myths of Indian Higher Education," *University News* (Novermber, 6, 1959). pp. 1–5.

[9] Soundararajan, Francis, "Curriculum of Colleges in the Twenty-first Century: A Paradigm Shift," *University News,* 37:39, (September, 27, 1999 ). pp. 1–5.

[10] Ghanchi, *Op.cit.*

[11] Kabir, Humayun, *Indian Philosophy of Education.* New Delhi: Asia Publishing House, 1961. p.169.

[12] Tyler, *Op.cit.*, p.12.

[13] Brubacher, J. *Modern Philosophies of Education*, New York: McGraw Hill Book Company Inc., 1962. p. 6

[14a] ———.Ibid, p. 350.

[14b] ———. Ibid, pp. 144, 164 and 187.

[15] Ghanchi, D.A. "Higher Education: Constraints and Strains," *University News*, (January 4, 1993), pp. 4–8.

[16] Kabir, H. Indian Philosophy of Education, *Op.cit.*

[17] ———. Ibid, p.170.

[18] ———. Ibid, p.171.

[19] Mascaro, Juan *The Upanishads*. Translation from Sanskrit with an Introduction, Maryland, U.S.A.: Penguin Books, 1965.

[20] Avinashilingarn, T.S. (ed.), *Education*: Sayings of Vivekananda, Coimbatore: Ramakrishna Vidyalaya, 1957. pp.7,8,11.

[21] Kabir, *Op.cit.*, p.172

[22] ———. *Loc.cit.*

[23] Vivekananda *Op.cit.*

[24] Varkey, C.J., *The Wardha Scheme of Education*. Chapter II: Gandhiji's ideas on Education, Madras: The Oxford University Press, 1939. pp. 77–82.

[25] Swami Prabhavananda and Frederick Manchester *The Upanishads*: Breath of the Eternal, New York : The New American Library of World Literature Inc., 1948. p.xi.

[26] Mascaro, J. *Op.cit.*, p.16.

[27] ———. Ibid, p.17.

[28] ———. *Loc.cit.,*

[29] ———. Ibid, p.18.

[30] Sen, K.M., *Hinduism: The World's Oldest Faith*, Hammondsworth (England): Penguin Books, 1965. p.65.

[31] ———. Ibid, pp. 66,67.

[32] ———. *Loc.cit.*

[33] Ibid, pp. 69–74.

[34] Nilakanta Sastri. *Op.cit.*, pp. 377, 378, 380–384.

[35] Jungalwalla,P.N. *Human Values in Zoarastrian Religion*, Bangalore: (Gandhi Center of Sciences and Human Values of Bharatiya Vidya Bhavan, 1988. pp. 11–20.

[36] Kabir. *Op.cit.*, pp.189–192.

[37] Krishna Iyer, V.R. Review of book: *Social Justice and Human Rights in Islam*, by N.A. Singh, New Delhi: Gyan Publishing House, in *The Hindu*, (Tuesday, November 9, 1999), p. 2.

[38] Nilakanta Sastri. *Op.cit.*, pp. 660, 661.

[39] Ganda Singh. *A Brief Account of the Sikhs*, Amritsar Siromani Gurudwara Prabandak Committee. pp. 2–7.

[40] These statements that seem to be of special significance to teacher educators of college teachers of home science have been starred.

# List of Readings

## BOOKS

**Avinashilingam, T.S (ed.)** *Education*: Speeches and Writings of Swami Vivekananda, Coimbatore: Sri Ramakrishna Mission Vidyalaya, 1971.

**Bharathi, K.S.** *Thoughts on Gandhi and Vinoba: A Comparative Study*, New Delhi: Concept Publication Company.

**Brameld, Theodore.** *Patterns of Educational Philosophy*: Divergence and Convergence in Cultural Perspectives, New York: Holt, Rinehart and Winslow, 1971.

**Brubacher, John, S.** *Eclectic Philosophy of Education*. New Delhi: Prentice Hall of India Ltd.

**Butter, J. Donald.** *Idealism in education*, New York: Harper.

**Carus, Paul,** *The Gospel of Buddha*, New Delhi: Publication Division, Patiala House, 1970.

**Cohen, Steven.** *The Philosophical Foundations in Education.*

**Dixen, Krith, (ed.)** *Philosophy of Education and the Curriculum*, Oxford: Pergammon Press, 1972.

**"Education and Traditional Values:** A Symposium", *The Education Quarterly*, Vol.XV, No.58, June, 1963.

**Franklina, W.K.** *Philosophy of Education*, New Delhi: Macmillan and Co., 1965.

**Gardner, J.N.** *Can We Be Equal and Excellent Too?* Delhi: University Book Stall, 1967.

**Garg, B.R.** *Lala Ralaput Rai as an Educationist*, New Delhi: Indian Publication Bureau, 1973.

**Karrupayail, Mohan, S.** "The Changing Educational Philosophy and the Left Out Indians," *University News*, 41:42, (Oct. 20–26, 2003).

**Kulkarni, S.N.** "Teacher Participation in Curiculum Planning and Development", *University News,* 39:31, (July 30–Aug.5, 2001).

**Mitra, Sisir Kumar.** *The Liberator: Sri Aurobindo, India and the World*, Delhi: Jaico Publishing House, 1954, pp.15–22.

**Munk, A.W.** *A Synoptic Philosophy of Education*, London: Abingdon, 1965.

**Nag, Jamuna.** *Raja Rammohan Roy: India's Great Social Reformer*, Delhi: Hindi Pocket Books, 1972.

**Navaratnam, Ratna.** *New Frontiers in East and West Philosophies of Education*, Bombay: Orient Longmans, 1958.

**Pandit Sukhlaji.** *Indian Philosophy*, Baroda: Good Companions.

**Patel, M. R.** "Commerce Curriculum in Higher Education: A Need-based Approach," *University News*, 41:49, (December 08–14, 2003).

**Phenix, P.M.** *Philosophies of Education*, New York: Holt, Rinehart and Winslow, 1958.

**Radhakrishnan, S.** *The Present Crisis of Faith*, Delhi: Hind Pocket Book, 1970, pp. 50–90.

**Rama Bai, S.** *Vinoba and His Mission*, Sevagram, Wardha: Akhil Bharat Sarva Sewa Sangh, 1954.

**Rayna, Ruth.** *Introduction to Indian Philosophy*: A Simplified Text.

**Rich, John.** *Martin Readings in Philosophy of Education*, California: Woodworth Publishing Company, 1968.

**Rosen.** *Philosophic System and Education*, New Delhi: Prentice Hall of India.

**Rusk, Robert, R.** *The Philosophical Basis of Education*, London: The University of London Press, 1962.

**Saiyidain, K.G.** *Maulana Azad's Contribution to Education*, Memorial Lecture (1960–61), Baroda: M.S. University Press, 1961.

**Schoffler, Israel, (ed.)** *Philosophy and Education: Modern Readings*, Allyn.

**Schofield, Harry.** *The Philosophy of Education: An Introduction*, Barnes and Noble Books, 1972.

**Seetharaman, A.S.**_*Philosophies of Education*, New Delhi.

**Shah, Beena and C.R.M. Rao.** *Tradition and Modernity in India*, Bombay: P.C.Manaktale and Sons Pvt. Ltd., 1965.

**Sharma, S.N.K.** *Madhva's Teachings in His own Words*, Bombay: Bharatiya Vidya Bhavan, 1979, pp.1–4 and 11–15.

**Sharma, S.R.** *Teachings of Gnanadeva*, Bombay: Bharatiya Vidya Bhavan, 1965. pp.1–7, 44–46 (Introduction and Conclusion)

**Sharma, S.R.** *Tukaram's Teachings*, Bombay: Bharatiya Vidya Bhavan, 1964. pp. vi, 1–7 and 58–60.

**Smith, P.G.** *Philosophy of Education: Introductory Studies*, Harper, 1965.

**Srinivasachari, P.N.** *The Wisdom of the Upanishads*, Madras: Sri Krishna Library, 1947, pp. Introduction and Chapter VIII.

**Strain, John Paul.** *Modern Philosophies of Education*, Random House, 1971.

**Swami Atmananda.** *Shankara's Teachings in His Own Words*, Bombay: Bharatiya Vidya Bhavan, 1960. pp. 17–29, and (Preface by C.P. Ramaswamy Iyer)

**Swami Harshananda.** *An Introduction to Hindu Culture: Ancient and Modern*, Bangalore: Ramakrishna Mutt.

**Whitehead, N.A.** *The Aims of Education*, New York: Macmillan Company, 1951.

**Wingo, G. Max.** *Philosophies of Education: An Introduction*. New Delhi: Sterling Publishers, 1974.

**Wright, B.A. Educating for Diversity**, New York: Day 1965.

**Yamunacharya, M.** *Ramanuja's Teachings in His Own Words*, Bombay: Bharatiya Vidya Bhavan, 1970. pp.1–55 (Section I and Section 11).

## ARTICLES IN JOURNALS AND NEWSPAPERS

(The following list represents a wide range of concerns and points of view expressed over decades, but it is not claimed to be exhaustive. More of these are read, more comprehensive and balanced may be one's understanding of the philosophical foundations on which higher education in India should be based).

**Bajaj, K.K.** "Human Rights and Higher Education," *University News*, 37:19, (May 10, 1999). pp. 1–5.

**Bawa, M.S.** "Educatonal Accountability: The Concept and its Implications," *University News* (September 4, 1995). pp. 9–6.

**Brenda M Gourlay.** "The Dangerous Faultline," excerpts from the convocation address at Vishwa Bharathi, Santiniketan, *University News* 36:32, (November 30, 1998). pp. 14–16.

**Chidambaram, R.S.** "Pursuit of Excellence" excerpts, convocation address *University News* 35:16 (April 21, 1997).

**Chowdhary, Karnala.** "Whither Gandhiji's Dream," *The Hindu*: Magazine Section, (May 25, 199). pp. 1 and 11.

**Clement, A.** "Humanistic Education," Education Supplement, *The Hindu* (September 21, 1993). pp. 19.

**Correa, Charles.** "The Philosophy of Life," excerpts from convocation address, *University News* (November 25, 1996).

**Das, B.C.** "Indian Society and Education in the Twenty-first Century," *University News* (June 23, 1997). pp.9–13.

**Deena Shah and Yeshpal Singh.** "Today's Youth and Gandhi," *University News* (Janauary 26, 1998). pp. 7–10.

**Dhillon, Jasvinder Singh.** "Educational Philosophy of Guru Nanak," *University News* 37:32, (August 9, 1999). pp. 6,7.

**Gandhi, D.A.** "Academic Freedom: The Fractious Scenario of Indian Higher Education," *University News*, (September 23, 1996).

**Gangrade, K.D.** "Building Moral Society Through Gandhian Education," *Journal of Higher Education*, 18:4, (August 1995). pp. 553–562.

**Jhalil, Rekshanda,** "An Indologist Looks Back," interview of Winand Catwaert, Research Director of Indian Studies, Department of Oriental Studies, Leuven, Belgium, in *The Hindu*, (Sunday, October 1, 1995).

**Kant, Sri Krishna,** "Towards Self-discovery," excerpts from convocation address at the Sixteenth Convocation of Sri Sathya Sai Institute of Higher Learning (Deemed University), *University News*, 36:4, (January 26, 1998). pp. 14, 15, and 18.

**Kazi, Bano Sartaj**, "Educational Contributions of Maulana Abul Kalam Azad," *University News*, 37:48, (November 29, 1999). pp. 9, 10.

**Lakshmanan, A.R.** "Education – An Unending Pursuit," excerpts from the Valedictory Address at the AIU West Zone Vice-chancellors Conference 14th October, 2000, University of Rajasthan, Jaipur, *University News*, 38:45 (November 6, 2000). pp. 6–18.

**Lipner, Julius.** "Hinduism and Hinduness," excerpts from talk on "Ancient Banyan and inquiry Into the Nature of Hinduness," Campus News, *University News*, (September 11, 1995), p. 35.

**Marmar, Mukhopadyaya.** "Management of Quality in Higher Education," *University News*, 38:27, (July3, 2000). pp.1–3.

———. "Taxonomy of Educatedness," *University News*,37:28, (June 28, 1999), pp.1–4.

**Narashima Rao, P.V.** "Gandhi's Relevance Today," *Journal of Higher Education*, Vol.18:4, (August 1995), pp. 547–551.

**Nath, K.P.** "Higher Education and Socio-economic Development," *University News,* (June 14, 1993). pp. 1–4.

**Om Prakash.** "Relevance of Education" *University News*, 36:32, (August 10, 1998). pp.1–3 .

**Parikh. Ramlal.** "Buddha and Mahavira on Education," *University News*, (September 22, November 25, 1991). pp. 12,13.

**Pylee, M.V.** "The Challenge of the Twenty-first Century," *University News* 35:36, (September 8, 1997).pp.15–22.

**Rai, Umesh Chandra.** "Cohesion of Culture and Indian Education," *University News*, 39:9, (February 26, 2001). pp.1–4.

**Rajput, J.S.** "Teaching is a Mission-Moulding Competent Professionals," *The Hindu*, Open Page, (May 8, 2001)

**Rangasamy, P.** "Universal Religion Already Exists," Vivekananda's ideas, Open Page, Supplement of *The Hindu*, (January 26, 1999), pp. 25.

**Rinpoche, S.** Presidential Address at the 73rd Annual Meeting of the All., on our university education – a critical view, *University News*, 37:7, (February 15, 1999). pp.1–5.

**S.R.** "Culture That Matters," Review in the Open Page, *The Hindu*, (December 15, 1998). pp. 28.

**———.** "Shepherd and the Philosopher," Review of Shrimad Bhagavatham, 11th and 12th skandas translated by Natesa Sastri and edited by K.N. Saraswathi, *The Hindu* Magazine Section, (Tuesday, July 22, 1977). pp. 26.

**Sarup, Anand.** "Functioning without an Institutional Ethos," *University News*, 36:42, (October 19, 1988). pp.4,5.

**Shanmugasundaram, Yashoda.** "Indian Education From a Colonial Toot of Administration to a Strategy of Social Development," 32nd Annual Convocation of Madurai Kamaraj University, Madurai, *University News*, 37:11, (March, 15, 1999). pp. 16–19.

**Sharma, Shankar Dayal.** "The Abiding Relevance of Buddha's Philosophy," excerpts from the convocation address at the Institute of Higher Tibetan Studies, Sarnath, Varanasi, *University News* (October 7, 1996)

**Sinha, S.N.P.** "Remembering Dr. Radhakrishnan," *University News*, 36:39, (September 28, 1998).

———. "Education for Excellence: Macauley's Mandate or Gandhi's Heritage?" *University News*, (April 27, 1998).

———. "Towards Inculcating Values in Education," *University News*, 39:43, (October 22–28, 2001). pp. 1–3.

**Trivedi, R.S.** "Gandhi – the Modernity of Tradition," *University News*, (May 11, 1998). pp. 1–3.

## RESEARCH PAPERS

**Association for Supervision of Curriculum Development.** *Criteria for Curriculum Decisions in Teacher Education*, 1963. Washington D.C.: ASCD.

**Babu, Burra Ramesh.** "Educational Ideology of M.K. Gandhi and Ivan Illich: A Study," Unpublished Ph.D. Thesis, Kakatiya University, Warangal, A.P., 1998.

**Chalam, K.S.** "The Changing Scenario of Higher Education: Coping with the Challenges of the Twenty-first Century," *University News*, Vol.41:28 (July 14–20), 2003, p.2.

**Chari, P.S.** "Identifying Standards of Exellence for Professional Education of College Teahers," Journal of Education Planning and Administration (Vol.XIV:4), New Dehli: National Institute of Educational Planning and Administration.

**Clement, A.** "Humanistic Education," Education Supplements, *The Hindu*, Tuesday, September, 21, 1993, p.19.

**Cronkite, B.** *Handbook of College Teachers*, Cambridge: Harvard Press, 1950.

**Devendra Kumar.** "Humanism and Theism: a study in Gandhian philosophy," Unpublished Ph.D. thesis Department of Philosophy, Benaras Hindu University, Varanasi, 1991.

**Jain, Saroj Bala** "Philosophical basis of contemporary social thought with reference to Gandhi and Nehru," Delhi University, Delhi.

**Max, E.** "Humanism, Education and Development: University Community link," *University News*, March 21, 1994.

**Puri, Binder** "Gandhi's conception of morality: A philosophical study," Department of Philosophy, University of Delhi,1998.

**Sengupta, Santwana** "Educational Philosophy of Sri Aurobindo and its implications on modern Indian education with special reference to international understanding and world peace "Department of Education, Rani Durgavati Viswa Vidyalaya Jabalpur, 1998.

**Sharma, Nripendra Nath** "Contributions of Sri Sankaradeva and his associates towards education amongst rural folk of Assam," Department of Education, Guwahati University, Guwahati,1988.

**Tiwana Pramjeet Kaur** "Educational Philosophy of Guru Gobind Singh and its impact on present thinking in education," Punjabi University, Patiala.

**Uberoi, N.K.** "Higher Education: the fate of Commissions and Committees – a Lesson for the Twenty-first Century," *Journal of Higher Education*, Vol, 18: 3, Autumn, 1988.

**Veeraraju, G.** "The Philosophy of Mahatma Gandhi and its relevance to the modern times," Department of Philosophy, Andhra University, Waltair, 1998.

**Verma, Anita** "A comparative study of the educational philosophy of Swami Dayanand and Shri. Aurobindo Ghosh and its relevance to modern Indian education," Punjabi University, Patiala,1995.

# Selecting Goals for a Curriculum

After laying down philosophical guidelines for selecting the goals of a curriculum, the next question is about what procedure may be followed in identifying the goals of a curriculum. The goals that are selected for attainment in an educational programme form the objectives of teaching and learning in the programme. For judging what objectives should be selected, Tyler has observed that "...certain kinds of information and knowledge provide a more intelligent basis for applying the philosophy in making decisions about objectives,"[1] and points out that no single source of information will be adequate to provide a basis for a wise and comprehensive decision about objectives to be selected.[2] He has suggested the following three sources of information.

a. Studies of the learners themselves,

b. Studies of the contemporary life outside the school,

c. Suggestions about objectives from subject specialists.

In India's educational system, the last stated source has been mainly utilized for setting up the educational objectives for any level of the educational hierarchy, while the other two sources are neglected.

Section 1

# Importance of the Three Sources of Information for Deriving Educational Objectives of Teacher Education

In the changing context of social realities and in the context of the continuing fall in standards of higher education, the college and university academicians and managements have had to surrender much of their administrative and academic autonomy to the State and Central Governments for managing higher education. There has been an ongoing debate as to the reasons for the loss of autonomy of the universities and colleges that has led to lack of control even over curricular issues.

Many other reasons apart, the academic autonomy of colleges and universities would be saved only when a high qualityof education of relevance to the socio-political needs of India can he ensured by educators and educational administrators, (See reference notes)

## 1.1 Importance of the Study of Contemporary Life as a Source of Educational Objectives of Teacher Education

For planning a curriculum at the higher educational level in India, the study of life outside the college or university claims priority because higher education is of great significance at the present stage of India's socio-political development. Higher education is expected to provide the much needed human resources in the kind of teachers who will be competent to meet the social demands on higher education. It is therefore important to study the contemporary society and identify the social needs, the needs of parents, and the government, as sources of educational objectives of a curriculum for teacher education to prepare the kind of teachers who will be competent to meet the social demands on higher education.

Many social organizations, the public and the intelligentsia through a range of communication media like journals, books, newspapers, radio and television; scientists, scholars and educationists through their conferences, and education commissions in their reports, have all expressed their expectations from college and university teachers. Their opinions and recommendations are sources of educational objectives of teacher education. The educational policy statements of the State and Central governments reflecting the aims of education form another source of educational objectives for teacher education.

Special educational objectives for the education of home science teachers can be found in the proceedings of the conferences held by the Home Science Association of India. From these proceedings, the long-term goals of teacher education for home science teachers may be stated, very broadly, as

> 1) preparing competent and committed teachers who would strive to achieve the socio-cultural goals in higher education in home science, 2) improving the professional competence of the practicing teachers, and 3) discovering more and more about the teaching-learning process and developing effective educational programmes in home science.

## 1.2 Study of Prospective Teachers as Learners for Identifying Educational Objectives of Teacher Education

Study of the learners as a source of educational objectives for a programme of education is important for planning a relevant prog-ramme. In teacher education the learners are the prospective teachers whose needs are an important source of educational objectives.

It can be assumed safely that in a course for preparation of college teachers, the learners will be fresh graduates and inexperienced unqualified teachers on probation. Such learners will come from differing educational backgrounds and varied professional experience. They will also vary in age and socio-economic status according to their backgrounds. Their aspirations and prospects, and the social context in which they would probably teach will also differ and influence their learning. There needs to be several surveys of the students with respect to these aspects, which will furnish the data from which the needs and goals of the learners can be identified.

Another source for identifying the needs of prospective college teachers to be taken care of is the information about and understanding of the service conditions of teachers in colleges and universities.

Research studies by graduate students in the subject of education and articles in social sciences in journals and newspapers too are a source of information as to the professional needs of college teachers. Such information can be found also in the papers presented at conferences of professional associations of Education, Psychology, Sociology and Home Science, and published in the proceedings of these conferences.

There is available a good deal of published literature on the problems of college teachers of India. It is, however, necessary to gather current information on the educational contexts, determined by the infrastructure, administrative, and other situational factors in which college teachers are obliged to teach. Information about the current socio-economic and infrastructure status of home science colleges and departments through surveys and questionnaires to college teachers and college alumni will provide valuable information for updating teacher education of college teachers of home science.

In short, teacher educators should be alert to detect the educational needs of student teachers. Comprehensive studies of students and teachers in service should be repeatedly undertaken so that currently relevant goals can be set for teacher education. While the philosophical basis and the implicit values of the subjects to be taught are relatively stable parameters, the socio-economic imperatives of a society and hence the needs of learners change with time and external events. Repeated assessments, therefore, of these two changing parameters are crucial for an effective and relevant programme of teacher education of college teachers, and in particular, of college teachers of home science, which is a subject dealing with a social unit under impact from changing socio-economic conditions.

## 1.3 Subject Specialists as a Source of Educational Objectives of Teacher Education

The major long-term goal of teacher education, as indicated by the expectations of the contemporary society in India, and by the professional needs of college teachers is the achievement of professional competency. The curriculum content of teacher education of home scientists will therefore include a number of competencies to be acquired for becoming a professionally competent teacher of home science in colleges and universities.

One source of professional competencies of teachers is their professional needs which can be identified by finding out what professional tasks college and university teachers face in teaching their subject and what competencies are required to carry out these tasks successfully. Data are needed from the community of college teachers as to their perceptions about what these tasks are, their relative importance to their overall effectiveness, and how problematic these tasks are. Such data will be an important source of educational objectives in teacher education curricula.

Professional problems of teachers and the professional competencies required to face their problems can be gathered from information in professional journals, newspapers, and other media supplied by social scientists and educators with professional and research experience.

❖ ❖ ❖

## Section 2 The Concept and Nature of Professional Competency as an Overall Major Objective

Extensive research into the nature of professional competency carried out in the United States, Canada, Britain, and European countries point to one conclusion: the definition of professional competency is complete only when it is defined in terms of abilities needed to cope with professional tasks in particular situational contexts. Also, mere possession of the required abilities is not enough, without such abilities being translated into effective behaviors that help to meet teaching and learning situations successfully. Professional education should therefore lead to change in the behavior patterns that indicate professional competency.

However, behavior patterns found to be effective in one particular context may not be so in another. Professional education should, therefore, emphasize on the ability to adjust behavioral patterns according to the teaching-learning situations teachers may face. It follows then that what is seen to be effective teaching behavior in pre-service education may not be so in the actual teaching situations that student teachers may face later.

According to Tyler, "...a profession is an occupation in which the specifies cannot be laid down,...." and hence the purpose of professional education is to develop in students behavior patterns that are not bound to a particular situation, and develop an ability to deal with new problems. Further, "...to go on being effective in new situations", 'concepts, skills, and values' can be used "...as a kind of framework for the educational programme as indicating behavior patterns that can be acquired that are not bound to particular situations."[4] It is advisable therefore, in choosing the objectives of teacher education, to focus on the stabler elements such as the abilities that are essential prerequisites helpful in choosing ways of being effective in new situations.

## 2.1 Some Models of the Nature of Professional Competency

Supporting the above ideas, there is a graphic description of a model of professional competence of teachers given by Robb.[5] He denotes teaching competence as that portion of an iceberg that shows above the water-line, with a supporting sub-structure underneath comprising of inborn physical and personality characteristics, the general culture and education of the individual in major areas of knowledge, mastery of tools of communication, reasoning, depth of insight into the world into the world around us, and some specialized knowledge. This means that the total professional competency of a teacher is like the whole of an iceberg, manifested in teaching competency like the tip of the iceberg needing the support of the substructure.

Biddle et al's[6] model for variables involved in teacher effectiveness research showed seven variables in a cause and effect sequence as illustrated below:

Formative – Teacher – Teacher – Immediate – Long Term<br>experience Properties Behavior Effects Consequences

They held that until effects desired of the teacher are decided upon, no adequate definition of teacher competence is possible.

Further, they distinguished 'teacher competence' from `teacher effectiveness', the former denoting the ability of a teacher to produce the agreed upon educational effects in a given context, the latter denoting the actual effects the teacher is able to produce. Both teacher competence and teacher effectiveness fall in the category of `teacher properties' in the model shown above.

Biddle et al also stated that teacher competence is not held to be composed of any single general ability or a fixed combination of abilities, but it is likely, "...that competence is that cluster of relatively unrelated abilities. Any one of these may be inappropriate in some contexts."

They stress the need to work out agreements at the national level on the educational effects the teacher is to produce, and commented that without such agreements no definition of teacher competence is possible.

When experienced educators discuss and arrive at recommendations as to the aims or abilities that should be the outcomes of education, they do so by drawing on the generalizations they have reached. Hence the recommendations of education commissions, professional associations, university Boards of Studies, and educators in their books, articles to journals, and research studies, form the sources of educational objectives broadly agreed upon by a large number of people. The abilities needed to achieve these broadly agreed upon objectives can be a basis for defining professional competence of teachers.

Going a step further beyond just competence, to the level of expertise in teaching, Lindsey expressed thoughts on a similar line, as given below:

> Expertness is to have specialized knowledge and skills required of all experts who are professional educators in teaching. Such knowledge and skills include those that take into account all the variables of any situation. Purposes of schools and the nature of learning experiences thought best to fulfil these purposes, and the roles of teachers in providing these experiences, may all vary in specifics from one situation to another, but can be treated at a level that will be inclusive of the differences, and hence will have. meaning for all teachers at all times in all places. Lindsey described 'expertness' in a practitioner as 'made up of, if not identical to', the discipline of education, and 'if the body of knowledge, those methods of discovering and

> verifying knowledge and those values peculiar to teaching' as elements of the discipline are defined, 'we would have a substantial foundation of the definition of expertness in teaching.'[7]

According to another expert body, though it is not possible to prepare teachers for particular teaching contexts, it may be useful to think of teacher competency with reference to certain teaching situations. This will be possible applying the suggestions of an expert body that the definition of competence should state 'what the teacher must be able to do.' and this may be derived from the role expectations held for teachers in their several professional roles.[8]

Each teacher educator should think afresh of teaching situations geared to the particular group of student teachers enrolled in a teacher education program. In the following pages a review is made, drawn from literature giving information on teachers' roles, role-functions, educational contexts and tasks related to role functions or in general, and the abilities underlying competency in these. As far as possible a good number of sources have been drawn upon to make as comprehensive a list as possible at the level of educational contexts and the three kinds of abilities: knowledge, skills and values.

# Defining Teacher Competency on the Basis of Role - Expectations for Teachers

There are numerous studies on the roles of a teacher and many categories of roles have been postulated in the research literature on role models of a teacher. There is also research literature on the role functions in each role that give an indication of the educational tasks chiefly involved in the situations described by the role functions. In any one of such situations, there may be one or more specific tasks to be carried out. Each specific task will be in relation to a specific educational context. Accordingly, competency may be defined as successful completion of a majority of the educational tasks identified for as many educational contexts as involved in the function of a particular role.

One approach, therefore, in preparing a curriculum for attaining teacher competency is to prepare a framework of teacher roles, identify the educational contexts and teaching situations and the educational tasks involved and set the educational objectives in relation to this framework.

## 3.1 Preparing a Framework of Teacher Roles of College Teachers of Home Science

For preparing a framework of teacher roles of home science college teachers the teacher educators of this group need to work together in universities and professional associations to identify broad but typical educational contexts that may be specific to a particular role or cut across a few roles of home science teachers, identify the educational tasks involved and also the abilities that most likely would be necessary for coping with these tasks. Again in such an analysis some tasks and abilities can be generalized to relate to several roles and contexts and some may be specific to a particular role or context or task.

Further, in the literature on competency referred to, it is seen that professional competency is thought to consist of two components: one, the *underlying ability* for effective behavior denoted as *potential* competency, and the other, performance that is effective, that is, effective behavior for attaining an educational objective denoted as *overt* professional competency.

In the professional education of teachers, responsibility can be assumed by teacher educators for developing potential competency of the prospective teachers, by focusing on developing abilities that are prerequisites to choosing ways of being effective as pointed out by Tyler, and which formed the stabler elements of professional competency. These prerequisite abilities," seen as stabler elements, have been stated as 'knowledge' in the form of `concepts', `skills', and `values' identified as related to abilities for carrying out an educational task successfully. The educational objectives of the curriculum content for the professional education of college teachers should therefore consist of items of knowledge or concepts, skills, and values required in the educational contexts found to arise in the professional roles of a teacher.

## 3.2 Literature Sources on the Professional Roles of a Teacher

A Commission on Teacher Education of the California Teacher Association identified six teacher roles, their major function and areas of teacher competence typical of each role. In outline the roles are: 1) Director of Learning 2) Counsellor and Guidance worker, 3) Mediator of Culture 4) Link with Community 5) Member of the School Staff, 6) Member of the Profession.[9] The report of this commission published in 1964 gives a description of the function or responsibilities and requirements for competence in each role with emphasis on what the teacher must be able to do rather on "how to do it".[10]

In a research study by Chari, definitions of teacher roles, role expectations, role functions and role tasks of each function, were identified[11] from fifteen sources of literature on teaching, the profession and the teacher.[12] On the basis of frequency of mention and importance given in the literature to the tasks, role function and roles, four roles, their role functions and tasks were taken up as the framework for classifying the identified abilities as needed for potential competency of a teacher in these four roles.

## 3.3 A Method of Identifying Abilities Constituting Teacher Competency

From sixty-three sources of literature on teaching and teachers, 675 descriptions of abilities needed in the categories of knowledge, skills, and values, important and basic to potential competency of a colleges teacher, related to the four selected roles, the role functions and tasks of a teacher forming the framework of reference described above, were collected.

In addition, through an open-end questionnaire, descriptions of knowledge, skill, and values, judged to be most important for the effectiveness of teachers were collected from ninety-one home economists of the United States and from thirty-four heads of colleges and departments of Home Science in India. Descriptions similar to those already gathered from literature were grouped together and integrated into single statements at the most specific level, and closely related specific descriptions generalized into broader aspects. By such integrative processes all the descriptions were integrated at three increasing levels of generality, namely, 'specific aspects', 'major aspects' and 'areas of competency' of a teacher role. These descriptions could be classified into six areas of competency in the selected four roles of a teacher.[13]

For validating the description of potential competency in the categories of knowledge, skills and values, a selected panel of experts who were educational advisors in universities, and 115 experienced college teachers of home science in India were asked to rate the descriptions on a rating scale of importance to effectiveness in a teacher. Those rated as important were selected as valid descriptions of potential competency in the four selected roles of a teacher[14]. This study provided a source of educational objectives for the curriculum of the professional education of college teachers. Professional competency as the main objective of professional education is reached when competency in the component areas of knowledge skills and values operates in a combination forming the ability to successfully perform the tasks related to a function relevant to a teacher role.

Though these descriptions of component knowledge, skill and value competencies were collected through study of an extensive range of publications, books and journals by eminent educationists and practitioners in the field, the sources were mainly from the United States. It was therefore necessary to explore sources that presented the opinions of eminent scholars and educational administrators in India, and the recommendations of the Education Commissions of the Government of India, for identifying components of potential competency of college teachers as educational objectives of a teacher education curriculum relevant to India. For this purpose, eighty-four articles on teacher education and higher education from educational literature in journals and newspapers published between 1990 and 2000 and beyond were scanned for statements on the concerns of educationists.[15] By grouping similar ideas and integrating them into generalizations, thirteen areas of concern were identified, which formed a source of educational objectives greatly relevant to teacher education in India.[16]

# Reference Notes

1. From "Autonomy of Universities in India, " by Gulab Gupta, *University News* Vol.42:11, (March 15–21), 2004. pp. 1–9.

   " 'University Autonomy' and 'excellence in Higher Education' were considered related by the national seminar of Vice-chancellors of accredited universities in India, ..."

   Prof. V. Subramaniam, Member, Planning Commission of India, "... emphasized the necessity of 'autonomy' in the working of universities without which 'excellence in higher education was difficult."

   "University Autonomy" was also discussed in the North and West zone Vice-Chancellors Conference, 1992 and in the 77th Annual General Meeting of the Association of Indian Universities, 2002, "where it was observed that the so called guidelines issued by the UGC from time to time not only restrict, but also erode the autonomy of universities," and also that "autonomy was endangered by large number of centrally created bodies ... as also by UGC directed curricula for 32 courses with the direction that universities should modify their curriculums and introduce the new system and this has led to loss of autonomy by the universities."

   "University education system in India has a constitutional base which deserves notice while considering autonomy and excellence in it". "The UGC is the statutory authority created by this law* as the instrumentality of the Central Government to promote 'excellence' in higher education system".

   *(University Grants Commission Act, 1956)

   "The UGC also has the authority to recommend to universities measures necessary for improvement of University education".

   "UGC now controls academics in universities and prescribe courses and syllabus."

2. From "Deregulation of the system of Higher Education," by Anand Sarup, **Journal of Educational Planning and Administration**, Vol.XIII:3, (July, 1999), pp.331–335.

   "The Education Policy of 1986 fully recognized the need for deregulation. That is why it advocated the dissolution of linkages between affiliating universities and colleges through the establish-ment of autonomous colleges".

   "In spite of these policy pronouncements, all institutions in the system of higher education are, even now, neatly arranged in a hierarchy. At the bottom are countless colleges whose voice is heard only during strikes and agitations. Otherwise they are looked upon as dumbnuts who know nothing and whose function is to do what is ordained by the affiliating universities. On the next rung of the hierarchy are the universities which lay claim to a precarious autonomy circumscribed by the national (UGC, AICTE, DARE etc.) and state level managers (State Councils) of these institutions".

"These apex institutions, even more than the universities, which have at least nominal revenues of their own, are completely at the mercy of the state and the central governments".

Asking institutions to 'put on a mantle of entrepreneurship,' is it feasible to achieve anything, "... if the general perception remains that whatever the intentions at the institutional level, nothing will happen without the approval of higher quarters?"

"Without taking measures for real deregulation to create the scope for autonomous and self-reliant innovations it would be unrealistic to hope for financial or functional support from trade or industry".

"Lastly, one must lay one more fallacy to rest. Just because universities or colleges get money from the UGC or AICTE or DARE, or even from the state government, it does not mean that the grantee institutions have to toe the line of the pay masters or withhold criticism, when it is due".

3. From "Does Performance Matter? Policy Struggles in Education," by Kuldeep Mathur, *Journal of Educational Planning and Administration*, Vol.XV:2, (April, 2001). pp.225–240.

"The policy process described above conforms to the general perception that educational decisions in India are political decisions and rarely reflected technical expertise in education. The political economy of education has remained a dominating factor in determining educational programmes," (pp.239) "... not focused on educational problems as technical problems, "... more concerned with political consequences of educational issues, ..."

The result is that a hiatus between politicians and experts has grown into negative mutual perceptions".

"A widely shared view is that education is fit only for academics and that politicians should keep their hands off'.

"But such splendid isolation made educationists blind to many aspects of educational reality which are basically political".

" ... because of this very isolation, the politicians remain largely ignorant of basic educational problems ..."

" ... educationists desire full political support without any political interference (which is their concept of autonomy) while politicians interfere too frequently with education (which is their concept of accountability to the legislature) without committing themselves to provide any support. (p. 240)

## References Cited


[1] Tyler, R.W., Basic Principles of Curriculum and Instruction, *Op.cit.*, pp. 3, 4.

[2] *Loc. Cit.*

[3] *Loc. Cit.*

[4] Tyler, R.W., "Concepts, Skills, and Values and Curriculum Development," talk given at Extension Curriculum Development Conference, Washington, U.G., (Dec, 8, 1963), pp. 2–5.

[5] Robb, F.C., "Post-graduate Development of Teaching Competence," Teacher Education: A Decade Ahead, report of the Dekalb Conference (June 29–July 2, 1955), Dekalb: N.E.A., 1955. pp. 296–301.

[6] B.J. Biddle and K.J.Ellena, *Contemporary Research on Teacher Effectiveness*, New York: Holt, Rinehart and Winston, 1964 ), pp.19–20.

[7] Lindsey, M. "Expertness in Teaching: Approaching to the study and Definition of Professional Competence," Report of the NCTEBS: Fort Collins Conference (Washington, D.C., 1962), pp. 99.

[8] Teacher Education Commission, *Six Areas of Teacher Competence* (Burlington, California: California Teachers Association, 1964 ), p. 17.

[9] Ibid., pp.12–15.

[10] Ibid, pp. 18–26.

[11] Appendix V: Chart of Analysis of Four Teacher Roles.

[12] Appendix VI: Bibliography of Literature on Roles of Teacher.

[13] P.S.Chari, "Identifying Standards of Excellence for Professional Education of College Teachers," *Journal of Educational Planning and Administration* (Vol.XIV: Nov. 4, Oct. 2000) New Delhi: National Institute of Educational Planning and Administration.

[14] Ibid, pp. 415–431.

[15] Supra, p. 48, Appendix III.

[16] Appendix IV.

# List of Readings

## In Curriculum Planning and Goals for Teacher Education in Higher Education

**All India Council for Technical Education.** "Documentation on Objectives, Structure and Policies and manual of Evaluation Procedure for Accreditation," *Journal of Highier Education*, Vol.18–2, (Summer, 1995) pp.310–319.

**Antony, Stella.** "A Strategy for Internal Quality Enhancement, " *The University News*, Vol.37:20, July 26,1999. pp.l–4.

**Bhatia, S.K.** "Personnel Function in 21" Century, "Management: Business Review Supplement, *The Hindu* (February 22, 1990).

**Chidambararn, R.** "Pursuit of Excellence", Extracts from Convocation Address *Universitv News*, 35:16 (April 21, 1997). p.16.

**Clement, A.** "Teachers' Role as a Creative Mediator" Education Supplement, *The Hindu* (Jan 4, 1990), p.18.

**Deshmukh, K.G.** "Universities and Higher Education in the

21st Century, *University News* (July 12, 1998), pp. 3–6.

**Dhagar.B.S and. Dhull, Indira.** "Some Reflections on World Declarations on Higher Education for the 21st Century," *University News*, 37:51, pp. 6–11.

**Dhesi, Avatar.** "Higher Education and Developmental Strategy," *University News*, July 18, 1994.

**Gautam, Mari.** "Quality Assurance in Higher Education: Criteria, Bench marks and Indicators," *University News*, Vol.37:42 (Oct.18, 1899) pp. 25,26.

**Gerth Donald.** "Education and National Development: Talk on Multi -disciplinary Approaches in Higher Education," *University News*, (Jan, 12, 1969) pp.4–7.

**Ghanchi,D.A.** "The Cyber Age, Education and the Teaching Profession,. *University News*, Vol.37:43, (Oct.25, 1999). pp. 3–6.

**Gopalan, K.** "Higher Education in India: Prospects and Perspectives, " *University News*, (Jan 9, 1995). pp.4–6.

**Handy, Charles.** "Middle aged School boys," *The World in 1995 – Leaders*. pp.19–20.

**Joshi, Anuradha.** "Value Development Among Youths – Vital Role of University" *University News.*

**Kapur, I.N.** "Teacher Training in Higher Education," *University News*, Vo1.29:25, (June 24, 1991) pp. 1,2,7.

**Kasturirangan, K.** "Education as Liberator," Excerpts from the Annual Convocation Address at the University of 13urdwan, *University News*, Vol.37:21 (May 24, 1999), pp. 13–16.

**Krishna Iyer,V.R.** "Priorities in Education, "Excerpts from the convocation Address at the 32nd Annual Convocation of the Shivaji University, Kolhapur, *University News* (April 22, 1996), pp.12–16.

**Kulandaiswamy, V.C.** "Higher Education Leads Towards Leadership," Address delivered at the Sixth Convocation of Manonmaniam Sundaranar University, Tirunelveli, *University News*, Vol.37:37, (Sept., 1999), pp. 13–16.

**Manu, Patrick.** "Total Quality Management in Education," *University News*, Vol.37:32, (Aug. 9,1999), pp.1–3.

**Meyer, A.** *Development of Education in the Twentieth Century.* Delhi: Prentice Hall, 1946.

**Mohanty, S. Behari.** "Professional Development of Teachers in Higher Education," *University News* (Oct 22, 1990).

———. "Excellence in Training of Higher Education Teachers", *University News* (Sept 8, 1997), p.5.

**Mukhapadyaya, M.** "Professionalism in Academics," *University News* (Aug, 1995), pp. 4–10.

**Nair, R.Ramachandra.** "History, Economics and Sociology of Higher Education in India," *University News* (March 21, 1994), p. 3.

**Nath, K.P.** "Education and Socio-economic Development," *University News* (June 14, 1993), pp. 1 & 2.

**Nayar, D.D.** *Towards.a National System of Education*. New Delhi: Mitthal Publications, 1989.

**Noorjahan, N.Gauhar and Shobana S.Nilover.** "The Need for Progessionalisation in Education", *University News*, Vol.36:57 (Dec 20, 1999), pp.1–5

**Pandey, Nithyanand.** "Researches in Teacher Education in India: Some Emerging Issues,' *University News,* Vol.36:3, (Jan 19, 1993), pp.9–11.

**Prakash, Ohm.** "Relevance of Education," *University News*, Vol.36:32 (Aug.10, 1998) pp.1–3.

**Pylee, M.V.** "The Challenge of the 21st Century," *University News*, 35–36, (Sept, 1997)

**Rai, D.K.** "Role and Responsibility of a Teacher," *University News*, Vo1.37:46, (Nov.15, 1999) pp. 5–7.

**Saha, Sujata.** "Quality improvement of Teacher Education: A Future Perspective," *University News*, Vol.37:37, (Sep.1999). pp. 6–9.

**Sant, B.A.** "Academic Staff Development in Higher Education," *University News*, Vol.37:19, (May 10, 1999). pp. 5–7.

**Santhana Krishnan, S.** "Teacher Effectiveness," *University News*, (June 27, 1992)

**Saraf, S.N.** "Higher Education and five Year Plans: Policies, Plans and Perspectives," Paper presented at the Administrative Staff College, Hyderabad, in *Higher Education in India: The Social Context*, *Op.cit.*, pp.265–286.

**Sen, B.N.** *Development of Education in New India*, New Book Society of India, 1966.

**Shukla, R.P.** "Quality Teacher Education Programme; Some Considerations," *University News*, 36:19, (May 11, 1998) pp.4–10.

**Singh, Amrik.** "Challenges of Higher Education," *University News*, (Dec 1, 1997), pp.19–22.

**Singh, B.K.** "50 Years After: Challenges Facing Teachers," *University News* Vol.35:4, (Oct 6, 1997) pp. 6,7 & 13

**Singh, Yogendra.** "The Dynamics of Social Change in India: Crisis and Resilience," New Delhi: Harvard Publications, Review in Open Page, *The Hindu*, Nov.30, 1993, .p. 23.

**Sodha, M.S., and B.K. Passi.** "Futures in Higher Education: Perspectives and Strategy," *University News*, (Jan 4, 1993). pp. 4–10.

**Soundararaj, Francis.** "Curriculum for Colleges in the Twenty-first Century" a Paradigm Shift," *University News*, Vol.37:39, (Sept,1999). pp.1–5.

**Srivastava, K.K., Mohindra, Sodha and Umesh Vashishta.** "Teacher Education in the 21st Century: Challenges and Opportunity," *University News*, (Nov.10,1997). pp.1–6.

**Takewala Ram.** "Emerging Perspectives and Paradigms in Higher Education," *University News*, Vol.35:20 (May 19, 1997).

**Tripathi, A.N.** "Ethics and Accountability in the Teaching Profession," *University News*, (Jan 23, 1991) p.1.

**Trivcdi, R.S.** "Indian Education and Education by 2000 A.D.," *University News* (June 14, 1993), pp.3 & 4.

**Venkata Reddy, K.** "Criteria of Academics Excellence," *University News* (Oct, 16, 1989), pp. 3&4.

**———.** "Towards a Socially Relevant Education," *University News*, Vol.28:28, (July 9, 1990), pp. 2–5.

**Venkataiah, N.** "Role and Responsibility of Teachers," *University News*, Vol.28:28, (Sept 2, 1991), pp.1–5.

**Verma, Shivendra, K.** "Issues in Higher Education," *University News*, (Dec 1,1997), pp. 19–23.

**Walia, K.**"Tasks Ahead in Teacher Education," *University News*, Vol.37:50, (Dec.13, 1999), pp. 13 & 14.

# Nature and Concept of Knowledge, Skill and Values as Abilities Forming Educational Objectives

Before setting up educational objectives in terms of knowledge, skill and value, it is important to understand the concept and the nature of each of these abilities. This will help in defining these objectives so that they are attainable through the educational process.

# Section 1 Acquiring Knowledge as an Educational Objective

For meeting knowledge objectives it is important to have a concept of what constitutes 'knowledge' as apart from information and knowledge as an educational objective of an educational program that can be evaluated.

The term 'knowledge' denotes, in a superficial sense, quantum of facts and figures, definitions, statements of principles and practices and other verbal expression of events. As an educational objective, 'knowledge' refers to the quantum of information that is acquired by a learner through the process of 'knowing'. The process of 'knowing' takes place at higher cognitive level than being merely aware of the existence of an object or an idea in the form in which it impinges on the senses, and is stored in the memory as information. "Knowing' goes beyond 'seeing' to the level of 'perceiving' by which the relationship between the new information and the already stored information is seen and the significance and implications of the relationship is also seen, giving the object or the idea a meaning.

The information which in this manner becomes 'known' is retained in the memory of the learner and can be recognized and recalled from memory. Such processed information is 'knowledge'.

In discussing 'knowledge' as an educational objective, Bloom et al.[1] identified a hierarchy of levels of 'understanding' or 'cognitive learning' and denoted the lowest category of' this hierarchy as 'knowledge' category. In this hierarchy, known as the Taxonomy of Educational Objectives, the knowledge category is defined as involving little more than remembering and recalling an idea or phenomenon in a form close to that in which it was experienced. The knowledge category may involve also relating and judging new information and relating it to knowledge already possessed so as to remember the knowledge already stored in the mind.

Distinguished from the above definition of knowledge are those conceptions of knowledge involving 'understanding', 'insight', or phrased as 'really know' or 'true knowledge'. The definitions of this concept of knowledge are closer to that of 'abilities and skills' in the Taxonomy of Educational Objectives.[2]

Knowledge is an important educational objective as it is basic to all other ends and purposes of education and is a prerequisite to development of intellectual abilities. Some knowledge is necessary for even manipulative and motor skills. Affective learning too, such as 'interest', 'attitudes', 'appreciations' and personal adjustments, is dependent on a foundation of knowledge[3] More information a person relates to an object or idea, more meaning or a better understanding of an object or idea is gained. More knowledge increases understanding of the nature of the object or the idea, moving closer to the reality of the material world. The pursuit of knowledge for the sake of knowing the reality of the world is a philosophical pursuit beyond the scope of the average formal educational system.

All information basis of knowledge cannot be held as complete or final or unchanging. Though all information does not remain eternally stable, it is assumed that a large part of what is known will continue to be stable and reliable for a long time. Still, the passage of time, geographical and cultural differences limit the knowledge of each group of people, so that knowledge of a particular period of time or culture is not the totality of knowledge possessed by the whole of humanity. Knowledge of anything should be held always as partial and relative rather than all inclusive and fixed.[4]

Knowledge, in a general sense, is defined as the totality of information preserved by culture, and 'information' is regarded as a phase of the process of learning which involves three stages: accumulation of material that may become knowledge, bringing acquired information into some logical order, and finally research.[5]

Knowledge is important as an educational objective only if it brings changes in cognitive behaviour, which may range from the simple behaviour of remembering and recalling to complex behaviour at the level of intellectual abilities and skills. The Taxonomy of Educational Objectives describes and explains the range of behaviours arranged in hierarchical categories from the simple and concrete level to complex and abstract level of intellectual abilities and skills.[6] In the lowest category labelled as the 'knowledge' category, the task for the individual in each knowledge test is to find out the appropriate signals and cues in the problem which will most effectively bring out whatever knowledge is filed and stored.[7] With the help of the Taxonomy the attainment of objectives as tested by behaviour can be ascertained by teachers and learners.

## 1.1 Kinds of Knowledge

Knowledge can be categorized in many ways depending on the purposes to be served. It can be categorised on the basis of objects such as persons, natural things or ideas; or according to how knowledge is acquired or to the degrees of particularity, or the date of discovery, place of origin and so forth [8]

Henderson refers to two kinds of knowledge: one, 'knowing that', for example, as knowing that coconut trees grow better in saline soil; and the second, 'knowing how' as for example, 'knowing how to use a spray pump or how to ride a bicycle, which cannot be described verbally but shown by action.[9]

Broudy categorized knowledge into three kinds: 1) knowledge in statements of facts, existential statements such as 'there is a cloud in the sky', an example of 'knowing *that* something or other was the case', 2) statements classifying things such as definitions and terminology which help in categorizing material to be understood and which may be called classificatory knowledge, that is, knowing *what*; and the 3) theoretical and explanatory knowledge or 'knowing *why*', which is the type of knowledge that is the most comprehensive of the three kinds.[10]

## 1.2 Concepts as an Important Form of Knowledge

It is difficult to recall from a large number of isolated unrelated items of facts a relevant item to understand new information. Items of specific sensory information are related to one another by perceiving the differences and similarities among them, and by abstracting the common characteristics, a 'concept' of an object, idea, or event is formed. A concept is an economic form of storing in memory a group of related items of information about an object, idea, or event.[11]

Concepts are formed in the mind as an image, an outcome of intellectual activities such perceiving, abstracting and generalizing. As such, concepts are both less and more than the instances or experiences from which they are formed. A concept is an image of a class of objects, phenomena, or ideas. Right from infancy numerous sensory experiences are discriminated, classified and generalized into concepts. The growing infant in due course of time forms simple concepts of 'light', 'bell', 'dog', 'crow' or 'orange'. These simple concepts with experience with more objects are further grouped and classified into larger concepts of a class of objects such as 'animal', 'bird', or 'fruit' and so on. The simple concepts are given verbal symbols or names like 'dog', 'crow', or 'orange', for the purpose of communicating.

These simple and larger concepts like 'animal', 'bird', or 'fruit' are termed single-term concepts. Such concepts are again combined to form more abstract concepts like 'wealth', 'justice', 'nation', 'democracy' and so on. Concepts, therefore, range from the simple to the complex and from the concrete to the abstract.[12]

Since concepts are formed in the mind of each individual, the concepts will not be exactly the same for all. However, by verbal communication of the concept of an object or on idea or an event, a group of persons may arrive at a consensus forming a group concept. This is why a verbal description of one's concepts is helpful in providing understanding within a group of people. In any body of information, numerous concepts, ranging from simple concrete ones to complex abstract concepts will be embedded.[13]

## 1.3 Concepts as Educational Objectives

The importance of concepts as educational objectives is stressed by Tyler in the following remarks:

> ...when you get into a profession, you are dealing with an occupation in which the specifies cannot be laid down because new problems arise and new knowledge becomes available to deal with these problems.

Pointing out that graduates from educational institutions learn to do precisely what the master did, Tyler asked " ... what is it that one can learn that will enable him to go on to be effective in new situations?" and answered that "concepts, skills and values can be used as a kind of framework for the educational program that can be acquired that are not bound to the particular situation." [14]

He further explained that 'understanding a concept is much more than rote memorisation', and that one needs to define it in his own words. Elaborating this, he said,

> He needs to be able to use the concept in thinking, in planning and guiding his actions. This depth and breadth of understanding takes time to learn. The reason it takes time to learn to understand and use a concept effectively is that the learner needs to work with a variety of illustrations of it. He has to have practice in applying each concept, seeing how it is used in a variety of situations.[15]

Tyler advised selection of a limited number of concepts in an educational program because it takes time to learn to use concepts. He gave the example of a group of physicists who recognized that basic thinking in physics rested upon some thirty-four powerful basic concepts as adequate for a high school curriculum, instead of three to four hundred concepts included in the usual program of physics!

## 1.4 Intellectual Abilities and Skills as Educational Objectives

As observed in the Taxonomy of Educational Objectives, though knowledge is an important outcome of education, it is not satisfying to regard it 'as the primary or sole outcome of instruction', but there should also be some application of the knowledge gained to deal with new situations and problems. For dealing with new situations, the necessary information and an appropriate technique for attacking the new problems that arise need to be selected. The ability for this is termed in the Taxonomy as 'Intellectual abilities and skills'. The most general operational definition of these abilities and skills is that the individual can find appropriate information and techniques acquired in his previous experience to bring to bear on new problems and situations.[16]

It is further stated that 'sometimes in educational achievement testing', 'intellectual abilities' are distinguished from 'intellectual arts and skills'. The latter calls for application of whatever general knowledge a person has, using a generalized method of dealing with new problem situations, in which emphasis will be on the mental processes of organizing and reorganizing material requiring 'little or no specialized and technical information'. On the other hand, intellectual abilities refer to situations calling for application of specific technical information to bear on a new problem, combining knowledge and intellectual arts and skills. However, since 'it is rather difficult to classify educational objectives and test items as abilities or as skills, without a full knowledge of the prior experience of students, the distinction is omitted in the Taxonomy of Educational Objectives. Hence, only the level of 'intellectual abilities and skills' is retained for educational objectives.[17]

The importance of setting up "intellectual abilities and skills" as educational objectives for our country lies 1) in the need for ability to solve independently personal and social problems of the present times, 2) in that the ability for independent problem solving indicates individual adjustment which helps in maintaining an independent personality as a citizen, 3) in that it indicates the maturity and integrity needed in a citizen as a member of the democracy to be an independent decision-maker, 4) in that they are more widely applicable than 'knowledge', having greater transfer value, and 5) in having greater permanence of learning .[18]

Educational Objectives in intellectual abilities and skills can be classified according to the hierarchical order of 'levels of understanding' provided in the Taxonomy, provided the mental processes involved and the behaviour outcomes are clear and specific enough to identify the order they can be related to. In general, in teacher education, such educational objectives should be set so that many intellectual abilities and skills are involved in reaching these objectives and these abilities are strengthened, improving teacher competence.

# Skills as Educational Objectives

When skills are set up as educational objectives, it generally, implies psychomotor abilities, though intellectual abilities also include skills, more in the category of intellectual skills. Klausmeier refers to two types of human abilities: cognitive and psychomotor. Cognitive abilities lead to learning of facts, concepts and intellectual skills while psychomotor abilities are:

> combinations of such physical factors as strength, impulse, speed, precision, coordination and flexibility, with such contents as body manipulation and object manipulation. The outcomes of learning associated with these psychomotor abilities are motor sets and skills.[19]

Any type of skill objective involves a knowledge basis, at least in the category of 'knowing how'. According to Broudy, skills have two major aspects: the 'executive' and the judgemental' described below.

> The former is a sequence of acts involving muscle movements or symbols or both. This sequence is guided by judgements (the second aspect of skill) in order to achieve some kind of adaptation.
> Skills vary in the required proportions of these components. The carpenter needs more of the judgemental factor than does a floor scrubber and the cotton farmer more than the cotton picker.[20]

With reference to skills as an educational objective in professional education, Tyler states that a distinction should be made between a highly specific skill that is greatly limited and a more general and significant skill, that is 'not likely to he outmoded ten or fifteen years after', and that 'in most professional areas we do find such skills'. For example, in law and medicine, 'skill in pleading before the bar' and 'helping a patient to feel at ease' are general skills respectively.[21] General skills, however, are 'learned through practice in a variety of specific situations' and can be in the nature of physical, social or intellectual skills. What are called 'skills' require 'more than just knowing how to do it', and doing it 'pretty well', 'easily and effectively'. Also, "in order to reach that level of ability, a good deal of practice is required, spread over quite a period of time"[22]

Klausmeier refers to a component factor of psychomotor abilities called the 'motor set', mentioned already, which referred to getting ready both mentally and physically at the neural level and deciding on proper stance and posture for taking action. Psychomotor abilities and physical activities seemed to mutually reinforce and enhance each other.[23]

Examples of building a mind and motor 'set' in our Indian culture can be seen in such activities like cleaning the house front entrance and decorating it with a 'rangoli' or 'kolam' as the first act on waking up, lighting a lamp before starting any special function and writing 'ohm' or 'sri' or any prayer symbol on top of an answer paper in examinations or of any document. Garlanding pictures and statues, or other holy symbols in shops and vehicles, and burning incense sticks, before starting the day's business, are all actions that serve to set the mind and the body for the work in hand, building confidence and hope for success. Start signals in races and team games also serve the same purpose.

In classroom teaching, the mindset for learning is brought about by such activities as taking attendance, writing the caption of the lesson on the blackboard, distributing lesson materials and asking a question to set the class thinking.

Evaluation of intellectual abilities and skills and psychomotor abilities can be done with the help of the Taxonomy of Educational Objectives, but only of the potential competency components for teaching and not for mastery of executive skills in performance in teaching, as mastery is gained through practice in the actual performance of educational tasks. Teacher educators, however, should display mastery of executive skills involved in their educational tasks thereby setting an example and also providing learning experience. Mastery in executive skills may be developed by new entrants to the teaching profession during their probationary period in junior posts in colleges, after they had acquired some intellectual and psychomotor abilities and skills in their preparatory education.

## 2.1 The Concept of Mastery in Knowledge and Skill and Its Evaluation

Mastery goes beyond 'awareness' to a high standard of precision in learning any material. Often, it is feasible to expect 'mastery' of basic knowledge, but only 'awareness and acquaintance' with major advanced knowledge in a field of study. A decision needs to be made while setting educational objectives whether only awareness is to be expected or mastery of knowledge and skill involved in reaching the objectives. This decision about the precision to be required of the student exists at all levels of knowledge.[24]

Since graduate students in professional education should already be having knowledge or information in a range of disciplines including social sciences at the level of awareness, they can be expected to aim at a high standard of precision and achieve mastery of the required knowledge or skill. The criteria for judging mastery over a whole skill or craft are the level of manipulative or executive skill, the time taken for the task, the number of errors, and the effort made: that is, the criteria of efficiency defined by the ratio of effort to results. The more complex the task to be mastered, the more important is the judgemental component as a factor in efficiency.[25] In a professional programme for teacher education with the main objective of developing potential competency in terms of mastery of skill, it is the aspect of judgemental component that can be evaluated in practice teaching sessions and though some evidence of executive skill will be available it will not be adequate to judge if mastery of a skill has been reached. The executive skill displayed will give to some extent evidence of judgemental skill applied to the task on hand.

❖ ❖ ❖

Section 3

# Values as Educational Objectives

The concept of 'value' is expressed as the 'worth' of an experience, or an object or an event. Judging the worth of anything that one comes into contact with is 'valuing', mostly done at a subconscious level, and is an intellectual process that goes on all the time. Value or the worth of anything is judged in relation to the importance of the object to the welfare and aspirations of self and society. A scholarly definition of a 'value' given by Kluckhohn is that

> a value is a conception, explicit or implicit, distinctive of an individual or characteristic of a group, of the desirable which influences the selection from available modes, means and ends of action.[26]

Morris distinguishes three aspects of the 'value field'. One aspect, called the 'operative values', refers to the 'tendencies or dispositions of living beings to prefer one kind of object rather than another', that is, the 'actual direction of preferential behaviour'. When preferential behaviour is directed by an anticipation or foresight of the outcome, 'conceived values' are at work. Here the object is conceived as preferable. If preference for an object is based on the properties of the object considered preferable or desirable, regardless of whether it will be actually preferred or is conceived as preferable, it shows object values'. In general the term 'value' refers to preferential behaviour.[27]

The Taxonomy of Educational Objectives in the Affective Domain defines value as an abstract concept of 'worth' as a result, in part, of individual assessment, but mostly for social assessment, accepted and slowly internalized as a criterion of 'worth'. The level of valuing increases with internalization and certainty, from the level of belief or mere acceptance to the level of preference and on to the level of commitment.[28] Tyler refers to values as the third level of human motivations, the first being that of primary basic needs, and the second, that of social needs.[29]

In a review of literature on the concept of value in behavioral sciences, four broad trends in the conceptualization of value were discerned by Nandy

as absolutes or independent validities,

as being in the objects capable of being appreciated or seen as satisfying a felt need by the subject,

as being in the valuer, as an internalized code or standard in terms of which selection is made in choice situations, and

as equated with actions, a concept supported by existentialists[30]

Nandy concluded that these different approaches were not essentially contradictory and not so exhaustive as to be mutually exclusive but dovetail, and hence it is more meaningful to treat Values as components of the individual's motivational system.

Hill and Dressel described what they termed 'intellectual values' as those which were intertwined with acquiring knowledge and intellectual abilities.[31] The category of 'professional values' indicates objectivity toward new ideas, conviction of the worth of every individual, and no blind acceptance of values held by people in power.[32]

A research study by Rana was made on professional values of home science teachers in colleges held at the level of commitment. Two kinds of professional commitment were hypothesized: one, predominated by 'value' for teaching or 'value commitment' and the other. 'value for interests extraneous to the teaching job itself, termed 'continuance commitment'. These two kinds of commitment were thought to he correlated and functionally fused together in behavior.[33]

Evidence of values lies in 'conduct', which is behavior considered 'desirable'. This is indicated by words or acts or any kind of expressive behavior, approval made explicit by word or deed, or by 'ought' and 'should' statements of preference made in daily behavior.[34] Expressive behavior indicating values are denoted as 'attitudes', defined as follows:

> an attitude is a learned, emotionally toned predisposition to react in a consistent way, favourable or unfavourable, toward a person, object or idea.[35]

In the Taxonomy Handbook II for Affective Domain, a classification scheme is presented in which categories of 'value' are arranged in a hierarchical order along a continuum of internalization from the lowest to the highest. The step in the development of a 'value' starts with 'awareness' of an object, idea or event and goes through five stages. The third stage, the level of 'valuing' is analyzed into the steps: 'acceptance' of value, 'preference' for a value or 'value-preference', and 'commitment'. Educational objectives of values as a dimension of potential professional competency can be evaluated in the form of 'value-preference' which can be verbalized.[36]

In setting up values as educational objectives, the background of values of students, their tastes and attitudes that may influence attainment of the selected value objectives need to be taken into account in evaluation of value objectives. The value-preference selected as objective should be related to the knowledge and skill objectives set up in the areas of competency identified as constituting potential professional competency of a college teacher. The value-preference expressed by students or cultivated in the program provides the motivational force for acquiring and applying the knowledge and skill components of competency in an area of competency. The three kinds of abilities are the dimensions of professional competency, which operate together to constitute potential professional competency of a teacher in an educational task.

The discussion presented in these pages on the concept and nature of the three abilities as components of competency have only skimmed the vast knowledge about these abilities that has been accumulated by outstanding educators and educational psychologists. The attempt here has been merely to acquaint teacher educators with some of the important basic thoughts of scholars in education. Teacher educators need to read the sources of literature cited as well as some of the 'readings' listed at the end of this chapter, so that they can gain a more thorough understanding of the concepts discussed here.

# Section 4 Defining and Stating Educational Goals

Earlier, it was mentioned that 'potential professional competency' of a teacher was the main goal of teacher education. The terms 'goals', 'ends', 'outcomes', 'purposes', 'aims', and 'objectives' are all used interchangeably in informal speech. Aiming at a stricter professional terminology, the terms 'aim' and 'goal' may be designated to mean a situation reached over a long period of time, after several intermediate stages of achievement of 'objectives' as short-term outcomes. For example, a broad goal such as 'professional competency' would be achieved by attaining several specific intermediary 'objectives' such as 'skill in communication' or 'knowing how to use an overhead projector'.

Long-term goals of an educational programme are difficult to check for their attainment. Any guidance that may be available from the evaluation of long-term goals will be at the end of a programme, by which time it will be too late to be of any use in preventing poor performance during the programme. For applying corrections in learning and teaching all along the way to keep learners on the right course, short-term intermediary outcomes should be set. Broad long-term goals should be broken down into their smaller parts to form short-term outcomes, or 'objectives', which can be quickly evaluated and timely guidance will be available for planning improvements in the course of an educational programme.

## 4.1 Stating Educational Objectives

It should be made possible to judge if an educational objective that signifies changes in behavior has been reached. It is therefore necessary to look for evidence of change of behavior that is expected or intended as an outcome of learning, indicating acquisition of new knowledge, abilities and skills needed for reaching a stated objective. There are therefore in a statement of an educational objective, two parts; one, to state 'what behavior' should change, and the other, to state 'in what' or 'with what', that is, the content, in which the behavior change is expected or intended to occur.

For example, if an objective in teacher education is for the teacher to 'develop ability in motivating students to participate in group discussions', the intended behavioral outcome (or change) is 'ability to motivate students' and the content in which this 'ability to motivate' is to be seen is 'participation of students in group discussion'. Taking another example: "skill in time management in preparing a meal", the behavioral outcome is 'skill in time management' and the content is 'preparing a meal'. Similarly in an objective for developing skill in effective communication with students during a classroom lecture, the behavioral outcome is skill in effective communication' and the content, 'a classroom lecture'.

The Taxonomy of Educational Objectives in the cognitive, psychomotor and affective domains offers help in defining and stating objectives in the areas of knowledge, skill and value, in such a manner that the fulfillment of objectives can be tested. Ample illustrations are given of tests for learning achieved in each class of taxonomy.

In summary, in this and preceding chapters, the first stage of curriculum development included, namely:

a. formulating an educational philosophy for the subject of study, that is, teacher education,

b. studying the three main sources of educational objectives of teacher education,

c. and deciding on a theoretical basis for identifying and defining the educational objectives of teacher education and the content of the curriculum.

It was stressed that the major aim of the programme of teacher education would be the development of 'potential' professional competency of a college teacher as an educator, and not as a subject specialist in a subject such as home science or economics etc. The subject content of the teacher education programme therefore is the discipline of 'Education' that includes major educational concepts, intellectual abilities and skills, and professional values involved in the educational process.

Curriculum development is not complete with identification done of objectives and the content, but includes consideration of the organization and the structure of the curriculum content. These aspects of curriculum content and the need for educational research by teachers in developing the curriculum are discussed in the following chapter.

## References Cited

1 Bloom *et al.*, *Op.cit.*, pp. 28, 29.

2 Ibid, p.32.

3 *Loc.Cit.*

4 *Loc.Cit.*

5 Tykociner, J.T., "Zetetics and areas of Knowledge", *Education and the Structure of Knowledge*, Fifth Annual Phi Delta Kappa Symposium on Educational Researcth, University of Illionois, 1963, edited by S.Elam, Chicago: Rand McNal1y and Co., 1966.

6 Bloom et al., *Op.cit.*, p. 28.

7 Ibid, pp. 28, 29.

8 Phenix, P., *The Philosophy of Education*, New York; Holt, Rinehart and Winston, 1958, p.48.

9 Henderson, K.B., "Uses of subject Matter," in *Languages and Concerts in Education*, (eds) B.C. Smith and R.H. Ennis, Chicago: Rand McNally and Company, 1961, p. 48.

10 Broudy,H..S., "Mastery and Types of Knowing" in *Languages and Concepts in Education*, *Op.cit.*, p. 77.

11 Klausmeier H.J., *Learning and Human Abilities*: Educational Psychology, New York: Harper and Brothers, 1962, pp. 155–164.

12 *Loc.Cit.*

13 Ibid.

14 Tyler.R.W., Talk on "Concepts Skills and Values and Curriculum Development", *Op.cit.*, pp. 2–5.

15 Ibid.

16 Bloom et al., *Op.cit.*, p.38.

17 Ibid., pp. 38, 39.

18 Ibid., pp. 40-43.

19 Klausmeier, *Op.cit.*, p. 33.

20 Broudy, *Op.cit.*, pp. 73,74.

21 Tyler, R.W. Talk, *Op.cit.*, pp. 6,7.

22 Ibid.

23 Klausmeier, *Op.cit.* 9, 226.

[24] Bloom et al., The Taxonomy, *Op.cit.*, p. 37.

[25] Broudy, *Op.cit.*, p.73.

[26] Parsons and Shils (eds), *Toward a Theory of Action*, *Op.cit.*, pp. 389–397.

[27] Morris, C.W., *Varieties of Human Values*, Chicago: University of Chicago Press, 1956.

[28] Kratwohl et al., *Op.cit.*, pp. 139, 140.

[29] Tyler, R.W., Talk, *Op.cit.*, p.9.

[30] Nandy, A., "The Concept of Value in the Behavioral Sciences," *Journal of Education and Psychology*, Vol.XX1I1, No.1. April 1964, Anand: Gujarat Vallabh Vidya Peeth, 1964. pp. 16–25.

[31] Hill, W.H. and P.L. Dressel, (eds), *Evaluation in Higher Education*, Boston:Houston and Mifflin Company, 1961. p.44.

[32] Tyler, Talk, *Op.cit.*, p. 9.

[33] Rana, Ansuya, "Professional Commitment of Home Science College Teachers in India, Its Relationship to Personal and Professional Characteristics and to Organisational Climate," Unpublished Doctoral Dissertation, 1981, M.S.U. Baroda.

[34] Kluckhohn, *Op.cit.*, p. 369.

[35] Klausmeier, *Op.cit.*, p. 254.

[36] Kratwohl, *Op.cit.*, p. 35.

## List of Readings

**BOOKS**

**Bloom, Benjamin.S., et al. (eds)** *Taxonomy of Educational Objectives*: Handbooks I and 11. New York: David McKay and Company, Inc., 1956.

**Hilgard, E.R.** *Theories of Learning*. New York: Appleton – Century – Crofts Inc., 1948.

**Klausmeier, H.J.** *Learning and Human Abilities: Educational Psychology*. New York: Harper & Brothers, 1951.

**Morris, C.W.** *Varieties of Human Values*. Chicago: University of Chicago Press, 1956.

**Parsons, T and E. Shils.** *Toward a Theory of Action*. Cambridge, Mass.: Harvard University Press, 1962.

**Smith, B.C and Ennis, RW. (eds)** *Language and Concepts in Education*, Chicago: Rand McNally & Company, 1961.

**Travers, Robert, M.W.** *Essentials of Learning*. New York: The Macmillan Company, 1963.

**ARTICLES**

**Devanathan, R.** "Valuing the Values," *University News*, 37:45, No. 8, 1999, pp. 15, 16.

**Gafoor, K. Abdul.** "Teachers as Professionals". *University News*: 38: 2–1, July 3, 2000. pp. 4,5 and 8.

**Goel, D.R., Chhaya Goel and Anshuman Das.** "Realisation of Liberal & Technical Education," *University News*, 39:17, April 23, 2001. pp. 11–13.

**Jeysala, V.R., Philomena Mary and S.Mohan.** "Facilitating Listening Skill," *University News*, 38:4, Jun 24, 2000. pp. 9–11.

**Kapur, J.N.** "Teaching = Lecturing / Evaluation," *University News*, 38:29, July 17, 2000. pp. 6, 9.

**Kirkman, Bill.** "Teaching Teachers to Teach," A Cambridge Letter, Magazine Section, *The Hindu*. Dec 9, 2001.

**Kumar Rajesh and Birendra Kumar.** "Instructional Skills of University Teachers, a study," *University News*. 36:47, Nov 23, 1998. pp. 11–13.

**Mashekar. R.A.** "Tomorrow's Knowledge Societies," Excerpts from the Convocation Address, University of Mumbai, *University News*, 27:8, Feb 22, 1999. pp.11–4.

**Oommen, Suman.** "Navigating Knowledge Meaningfully," Education: Open Page, *The Hindu* Oct 16, 2001.

# Developing the Curriculum

The term 'Curriculum', in ordinary parlance, is taken to mean the 'syllabus' of an educational program. In this chapter, a broader concept of the term is discussed. Further, in addition to a philosophy of education, and selection and statement of objectives, other elements, such as the content, provision for learning, and evaluation of learning, needed to make a program operational, are also discussed.

# The Concept of Curriculum

The term 'curriculum' is a familiar one for teachers and educationists and even for the educated lay public. However, educators require, or should require, a correct and shared understanding of the term in its technical sense as applied in Education as a distinct field of knowledge. The present popular concept of a curriculum is seen in the 'syllabus' consisting of an outline of topics under which information to be given to the students is prescribed. The term 'curriculum' is perhaps discussed in a course of study on planning lessons in a teacher education programme, but in practice the term hardly refers to anything more than the 'syllabus': that is, a body of information presented in outline under a series of topics, logically classifying the information in a subject of study.

The teacher is expected to expand the topical outline by filling in the factual details of information. For this purpose, more often than not, the teachers take recourse to 'following' a textbook written by selected authors and plan their lessons to 'cover' the syllabus using the information in the textbooks. Far different from this concept of the curriculum is the concept of the curriculum describing it as comprising of all planned learning experiences intended to bring about changes of behavior in selected desirable ways set up as objectives. This concept includes guidance of learning experiences for acquiring relevant knowledge, skills and values related to the objectives of the curriculum.

## 1.1 Two Main Aspects of a Curriculum

The two main aspects of a curriculum are: the content, and the scheme of organization of the content. The curriculum content consists of objectives, learning experiences, information or 'subject matter' thought to be necessary for reaching the objectives and the evaluation plans made to check if the intended learning did take place or how far the learning went.

The second aspect, the organization of the curriculum, has to do with the ordering or arrangement of the content of a whole course of study over a period of time, like one year or two years or six months. A course of study may consist of units of study, or a short course of study centered around a major theme, issue or problem or a project. After objectives are selected, organization is an important aspect to be considered. It is important because the objective of change of behavior can be brought about mainly through the cumulative effect of several learning experiences organized according to certain principles of organization and the structure of subject-matter. Tyler gives this picturesque description of the effect of organizing learning experiences:

> In some respects educational experiences produce their effects in the way water dripping upon a stone wears it away. In a day or a week or month there is no appreciable change in the stone, but over a period of years definite erosion is noted. Correspondingly, by the cumulation of educational experiences profound changes are brought about in the learner.[1]

An old Tamil proverb says, on the same lines, that 'even a stone over which there is a constant traffic of ants gets worn down in time'.

## 1.2 The Concept of Structure in the Curriculum Content

Basic to the step of organizing a curriculum are the questions as to 'what should be taught, when, and how' Leading scientists, mathematicians, psychologists and historians as well as educators, in a major effort at curriculum designing in the United States, after decades of debates and discussions, focused on the design of a curriculum in which subject matter would be presented effectively. Such a design meant that due regard was given not only to 'coverage' of the content but also to the 'structure' of the subject.[2]

The meaning of 'structure' in a subject is the way things are related.[3] One question is "What are the implications of emphasizing the structure of a subject, be it mathematics or history – emphasizing it in a way that seeks to give a student as quickly as possible a sense of the fundamental ideas of the discipline?"[4]

It is seen that emphasis on structure stimulates students in the learning process[5] and therefore it is central to good teaching.

> The teaching and learning of structure, rather than simply the mastery of facts and techniques, is at the center of the classic problem of transfer, and if earlier learning is to render later learning easier, it must do so by promoting a general picture in terms of which the relations between things encountered earlier and later are made as clear as possible.[6]

Two ways in which learning serves the future, Bruner explains, is through 1) specific transfer of training and 2) non-specific transfer: that is, transfer of principles and attitudes. The continuity of learning produced by transfer of principles and attitudes, that is, learning initially not a skill but a general idea, is dependent upon mastery of the structure of subject matter, which means having an idea of the general nature of the phenomenon being studied. "The more fundamental or basic is the idea, almost by definition, the greater will be its breadth of applicability to new problems," and the problem is how to construct curricula and revamp text and teaching materials so that 'pervading and powerful ideas and attitudes' are given a central role in the subject matter of a discipline, and how match the levels of teaching materials to different levels of abilities of students.[7]

Somewhat similar to this idea is Tyler's proposition of the idea of elements in a curriculum that serve as organizing threads for preparing a plan of organization of a curriculum.[8] For example, the organizing elements in mathematics are such basic concepts as the 'place value of a number system', and some basic skills like the ability to solve problems involving common fractions. Similarly, the concept of interdependence of peoples is a widely used concept that may start at the level of the primary class children who are made to see their dependence on the milkman for getting milk and the same concept grows broader and deeper at the high school level where international independence in trade can be seen.[9]

These elements that serve as threads give continuity, sequence and integration to a curriculum. A teacher education curriculum designed to give continuity, sequence and integration will promote better understanding, greater retention, and wider transfer of principles and attitudes involved in the educational process. In organizing learning experiences the structure of subject matter as expounded by the above two scholars will form an important basis.

## 1.3 Organizing Learning Experiences

Learning Experiences are an important aspect of a curriculum content because they are intended to promote learning of the concepts, skills and values that will bring about the changes of behavior leading to fulfillment of selected objectives. Learning experiences, to be effective in promoting intended learning, need to be organized based on the relationships of learning experiences that are involved in moving towards reaching intended educational objectives.

They maybe organized on the basis of relationship over a time period or from one area of subject matter to another. The former type of relationship is referred to as 'vertical' relationship and the latter as 'horizontal'. When learning experiences in a subject at a lower class or level are related to learning experiences at a higher level in the same subject, it is seen to be vertical organization. If learning experiences in one subject at one level are related to those in another subject at the same level or class, it is horizontal organization. Both kinds of organization reinforce learning in different ways. Vertical organization gives greater depth and breadth of understanding a problem and horizontal organization gives greater understanding of the significance and unity of view regarding a problem or issue studied.[10]

For example, human dwellings, clothing and food, may be studied with greater and greater scientific and technological depth from one year to another, through vertically organized learning experiences. They may also be studied, at the same time, from economic, cultural and geographic points of view or in relation to management or child development or sanitation and health at every level or class, through horizontal organization of learning experiences in these different subjects.

Effective organization of learning experiences should satisfy three major criteria: **continuity, sequence** and **integration**. The important elements of content for which learning experiences are organized are concepts, skills and values embedded in the content. 'Continuity' in the content refers to giving recurring learning opportunities for learning selected concepts, skills and values through effective vertical organization. 'Sequence' in the organization of learning experiences refers to providing increasing levels of learning of a concept, skill or value, with each learning experience. 'Integration' in the organization of learning experiences is brought about by providing learning experiences that promote an understanding of the horizontal relationship of a concept, skill or value, across different fields of study or different situations. Horizontal integration should show how the same concepts, skills and values are involved in many branches of study, and not as isolated behavioral outcomes of a single course of study.[11]

Some concepts, skills and values are so basic to human development and social progress that they pervade learning at all levels and in all fields of learning. For example, the concept of human interdependence, man and environmental interdependence, numeracy skills, and value for life, are some of the underlying elements integrating the whole content of a curriculum, and therefore should be taken into account in developing a curriculum.[12]

Curriculum development is an exercise in the economics of making judicious choice of educational content within the limitations of resources such as the abilities and socioeconomic resources of students, availability of student time, infrastructure facilities of educational institutions and financial and civic resources of the community.[13]

Section 2

# Developing the Curriculum Content

The curriculum content is the other main aspect of a curriculum along with organization that has been discussed above. It has been mentioned that the curriculum content consists of objectives, learning experiences and the evaluation plans to assess the success of the curriculum. The concept of educational objectives has been discussed in the earlier chapter. An important criterion setting up educational objectives was, it was stated, the scope for evaluating the fulfillment of the stated objectives. An objective that cannot be evaluated with respect to the attainment of the objective would not be useful as an educational objective.

There may be, of course, a few widely held group values set up as objectives, because of their significance to personality development or to the society's welfare, even though they cannot be evaluated. Apart from these, the evaluation of attainment of nearly all the educational objectives is important in judging the success of an educational programme. Evaluation process has also a role to play in the development and implementation of the curriculum of an educational programme. Besides evaluation, learning experiences are also another important element in developing a curriculum. In the following pages the concepts and the role of evaluation and learning experience are described.

## 2.1 The Concept and Role of Evaluation in Education

Generally, evaluation is thought to be a process called for at the end of a period of education for judging the success of students against the criterion of pass marks accepted in the educational system. This evaluation is made in the terminal examinations, with reference to the syllabus prescribed for an education programme, to test the learning achieved of the subject matter given in the syllabus. Rarely is evaluation thought of in relation to educational objectives in the form of knowledge as understanding, of skills and of values. In the first place, such objectives are not set up in the curriculum of an educational programme, in the current educational setup.

This is the situation mostly prevailing in the Indian system of education from the school to postgraduate levels. But under the broader concept of an educational curriculum described in the foregoing pages, in teacher education, prospective teachers need to learn how to select and state programme objectives so that they can be evaluated, applying such models as presented in the Taxonomy of Educational Objectives or in any other scholarly texts.

Evaluation of teaching and learning is an integral part of the educational process and is considered inevitable, in the modern concept of evaluation. Dressel, writing on the inevitability of evaluation' says

> ... education is a complex process involving the selection of ideas (concepts, values, skills) and the planning of experience designed to foster mastery of these ideas in the people subjected to the educational process. Choices must be made in planning an educational program, and the effectiveness of the program must also be studied. Evaluation is therefore, inevitable in education when one is faced with choice, evaluation, whether conscious or not, is present.[14]

Further, he states that evaluation is both a means and an end.

> As a means it includes studies and procedures designed to maintain or improve the quality of instruction or of learning. Tests, grades, student opinionnaires for apprising teaching, and intricately planned research studies – all are or may be means to assess and possibly to raise the quality of teaching.[15]

Stating that 'evaluation' is also an end or a goal, Dressel points out that 'evaluation' is the 'culminating category in the hierarchical ordering of cognitive objects', requiring judgement. This judgement is evaluation in decision-making, but evaluation is also a process of reaching a judgement, implying this ability to evaluate. Engaging in evaluation, as process becomes the educational goal.[16]

If the evaluative process showing a thoughtful and analytical approach to decision-making is followed by the faculty and the administrators of educational institutions, it provides a model to the public, and an environment in which students learn how wise judgement can be made by observing and participating in the process.[17] "Evaluation and the learning process are interrelated," in learning to exercise critical judgement, in determining the effectiveness of learning and also in self-appraisal.[18] "To the extent that evaluation processes are consistent with known principles of learning, evaluation can contribute to learning," states Saupe, who has devoted a whole chapter to discussing the nature of the integration of the evaluation and learning processes.[19]

A brief reference to the many ways in which evaluation is crucial to the learning process as discussed by Saupe is made here. Application of the evaluative process is required for

judging readiness for learning,

bringing clarity of goals that provides motivation to learn,

emphasizing organization and meaning by giving attention to generalizations and principles that need to be identified,

providing active involvement in learning,

confirmation or reinforcement of learning through feedback,

providing a test of transfer of learning showing the ability to apply learning to new situations,

critical thinking and

changing of attitudes[20]

Evaluation therefore also helps in teaching, in improving the curriculum or course content, to gain the understanding and cooperation of students when they see, through self-evaluation and continuous evaluation, how they are progressing, and by making students feel responsible for their own learning.[21]

The above discussion on evaluation is by no means exhaustive or in depth in regard to the knowledge available and increasing among scholars in education. The effort made here has been mainly to make teacher educators aware of the importance of the role of evaluation and the concept of evaluation in Education. A list of some of the valuable publications on evaluation is given at the end of this chapter. Teacher educators and student teachers should become familiar with at least one publication and be aware of the kind of help available from a few others. Learning about evaluation should continue throughout a teaching career to keep on improving the quality of education.

## 2.2 The Concept and Role of Learning Experience

Learning occurs through experience, but not all experiences lead to learning. Any experience is not a 'learning experience' unless the learner comes to know something more than before. The term 'learning experience' refers to the interaction between the learner and the external conditions to which he can react. Further, as Tyler stated,

> The essential means of education are the experiences provided, not the things to which a student is exposed.
>
> This definition of experience as involving the interaction of the student and his environment implies that the student is an active participant, that some features of his environment attract his attention and it is to these that he reacts.[22]

Learning experiences in a curriculum are planned so that they lead to attainment of the objective set up. There are five elements involved in providing a learning experience:

1. the subject matter or whatever is to be learnt,
2. where or in what context or situation is the learning experience to be provided,
3. by what means and materials the experience is to be presented,
4. the teacher, and
5. the learner,

When all the above five elements are present and interact or operate, a 'learning experience' is provided. An effective learning experience requires focus on the learner, relating all the other elements to the needs, interests, attitudes and abilities of the learner, and stimulating active interaction.[23] Learning experiences may range from a glimpse or sensation of a situation to overtime involvement in an ongoing process, and which may be intellectual, psychological, physical, social, political or economic in nature.

Even if a learning experience is planned for a group and is shared, there would be differences in the learning achieved by individual members and all will not learn the same thing to the same extent, due to individual differences.[24] One learning experience may not be adequate to lead to the objective for which it is planned, but more than one experience may be needed to gain the kinds of learning leading to an intended objective. Also, a learning experience may not lead to only the intended objective but to many other kinds of learning leading to other objectives.[25]

When objectives imply changes of behavior, there are particular characteristics of learning experiences for attaining a particular type of objective, say, 'skill in thinking', 'acquiring functional information', 'developing social attitudes', 'developing interest', and so on.[26]

Understanding fundamentals in concepts, skills and values requires much time and many educational experiences, because only their cumulative effect can be expected to change behavior implied in the objectives set up. For a cumulative effect, learning experiences need to be organized to give 'continuity' by reiterating the concepts, skills and values introduced, known as vertical organization and to bring in 'sequence' of learning by having each successive experience build upon the preceding one, going more broadly and deeply into the matters involved. By organizing learning experiences for acquiring concepts, skills and values in one subject their application in other fields of study, providing a horizontal relationship of learning across different subjects, 'integration' of a curriculum content is achieved.[27] Learning experiences are important for making a curriculum operational and an education programme successful.

'Evaluation' and 'learning experience' are two major processes important in preparing the curriculum content for teaching. They are important because 1) the selection of educational objectives should be on the basis of the possibility of providing learning experiences for attainment of the objective and evaluating the attainment, 2) the two processes are pervasive throughout teaching in an educational program and are closely interrelated.[28]

## 2.3 Some Other Pervasive Processes Important in Implementing a Programme of Education

'Communication' is an important process for effective implementation of an education programme. It is basic to bringing about the interaction of learners with the teacher, the subject, material aids and the context or the learning situation. It is interaction through communication that provides the learning experience by which motivation to learn can be built up.

Another important process is 'management' of the teaching-learning situations and learning experiences, to give direction and control over the educative process. Management also implies 'supervision' as a means of guiding learners and involves 'planning' the learning experiences and the learning situations. Understanding these pervasive processes call for scholarship in their theoretical foundations and for effective teaching, development of skill in application of these processes.

❖ ❖ ❖

# Section 3 The Concept of Educational Research and the Role of Research in Developing the Curriculum in Teacher Education

Even if it is accepted that mastery of knowledge in a subject specialist is a part of the competency of an educator that alone is not adequate to become an effective teacher. Specialization in the discipline of Education too is necessary to become a competent educator in any branch of knowledge. It should also be recognized that the professional teacher education programme is only a preparation for becoming an educator and provides only a foundation for keeping on improving in professional competency.

However, it implies that opportunities for improving exist in the educational system of the country, and that the necessary administrative attitudes as well as the resource infrastructures exist at the college and university levels. For continuous professional growth as an educator, such factors as an easily accessible library, well stocked with up-to-date books and journals, time to spend on reading and experimenting with new ideas within the scheduled work time, and autonomy to develop courses of study, should be available to teachers.

Not only teachers who teach Education as a subject but also specialists in other disciplines need to carry on some research in the educational aspects of the subjects they teach. Time for all teachers for some research into the problems of teaching their subjects should be treated as a legitimate use of time in the work schedule of teachers. Minor research studies by teachers in service, in the educational aspects, would add to the growth of knowledge about the educative process and ways to improve the quality of education.

A popular concept of research implies that hours are spent in the seclusion of libraries examining documents and books or in doing experiments in laboratories. Sometimes, research is thought to be collecting a mass of data available on some object or event. Often, research is considered only for getting an academic degree, or for improving a teacher's professional bio-data record so as to qualify for a promotion in salary or rank. But for improving teaching and the quality of education offered in colleges only research by the teacher on the concepts, skills, abilities and values and the methods and materials of teaching, to effectively face the educational tasks will be useful. Such useful research can be planned by a teacher by selecting an educational problem to be solved or any question that needs an answer, or making a better impact on the students through better planning of a learning experience.

The teacher's research may range from a very narrow specific question related to any one of the five elements of teaching-learning situation mentioned earlier.[29] requiring a short period of time, to larger aspects of teaching such as the effectiveness of certain methods or teaching aids, which may take a long time. Data for teacher research can be collected during the usual schedule of class sessions as a part of the teaching learning process.

The important aspects of such research are defining the problem in terms of specific variables or characteristics, deciding what data would be relevant that can be collected in the course of a class session as a part of the teaching-learning process, making a systematic collection of accurate data, perhaps sustained over a period of time and proceeding to classify and analyze the data later on. Records of useful data will be available with the department office in the form of bio-data of students enrolled and the achievement records in tests and examinations, as additional data to the data collected during classroom research. A model for such research in which each class session can be planned as a research situation is presented and discussed in an article as described below.[30]

## 3.1 A Spiralistic Conception of an Educational Research Model

The author of the article on educational research states that educational research is operational research that refines and reformulates rather than make discoveries. He suggests a conceptual model of educational research, systematically integrating theoretical, empirical and practitioner components. The author's opinion underlying the model is that educational research "... is or ought to be an interplay of activity involving the continuous interplay of the conceptual, empirical and practical dimensions."[31] The model, diagrammatically shown in figure represents a spiralistic conception of an educational development model structured in terms of the activities involved.

As shown in the diagram, the whole purpose of the exercise is to refine $H_1$ and hence S and C. The T phase operates at two levels: $T_1$ being as near the ideal situation as possible but not truly laboratory conditions, should move to $T_2$ through a series of testing situations. $T_2$ is the non-ideal (real life) situation, normal operating conditions. The research phase of $T_2$ is conceived as a form of action research.

The author argues that educational innovations are not inductively generated by research or practice but more by informed guesses and conjectures. Research and practise structure, and refine ideas prior to and during implementation: For making adequate attempts to structure and refine ideas prior to and during implementation, use is made of an 'error eliminating' procedure for progressive development of educational ideas and theories. The model shows action research that can be attempted in the day-to-day work of the teacher under normal operating conditions. According to the author, educational research has not benefited significantly from research but such research as described above will benefit educational practice.

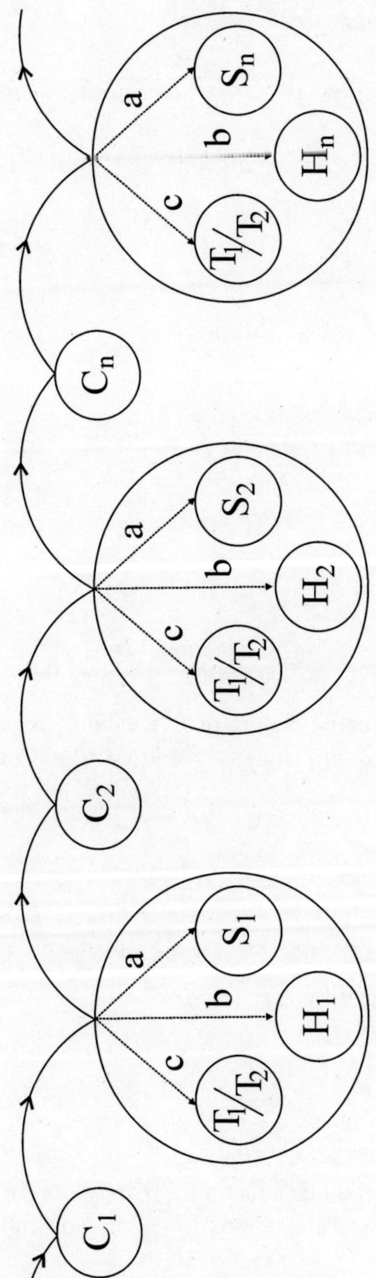


$C_1C_2 \ldots C_n$ Sequence or set of Conjectures which may or may not be cumulative

$S_1S_2 \ldots S_n$ Systematic theoretical formulations derived from C

$H_1H_2 \ldots H_n$ Tryable or testable hypothesis exemplifying some aspects of or derived from S

$T_1T_2 \ldots T_n$ Testing situations, but more after experiential trials or experimental tests

## References Cited

[1] Tyler, R.W. *Basic Principles of Curriculum Construction and Instruction. Op.cit.* p.54.

[2] Bruner, J.S. *The Process of Education* Cambridge, Mass.: Harvard University Press, 1962. p. 2,3.

[3] Ibid, p.7.

[4] Ibid, p.3.

[5] Ibid, p.8.

[6] Ibid., p.12.

[7] Ibid., pp. 17 & 18.

[8] Tyler, R.W. Basic Principles... ., *Op.cit.* p.56.

[9] *Loc. Cit.*

[10] Ibid., pp.54–57.

[11] Ibid., pp. 55, 56.

[12] Ibid., p. 57.

[13] Phenix, P. *The Philosophy of Education*, New York: Holt, Rinehart, and Winston, 1958. pp. 58–60.

[14] Dressel, Paul L. "The Essential Nature of Evaluation," *Evaluation in Higher Education*, Boston: Houghton and Mifflin Company, 1961. p. 6.

[15] Ibid, pp. 24,25.

[16] Ibid, pp. 25,26.

[17] *Loc. Cit.*

[18] Saupe, Joe I. "Learning and Evaluation Process" Chap.3, *Evaluation in Higher Education, Op. cit.* p. 54

[19] *Loc. Cit.*

[20] Ibid, pp. 54,57.

[21] Ibid.

[22] R.W. Tyler, Basic Principles... , *Op.cit.*, p. 41.

[23] J.P. Leagans, Setting up learning Situations," *Extension Education in Community Development* Publications Division, Government of India, New Delhi, 1960.

[24] Tyler, *Op.cit.*, p.41.

[25] Ibid., pp. 42–44.

[26] Ibid., pp.44–53.

[27] Supra, p. 97.

[28] Supra, p.100

[29] Supra, p.102.

[30] Eastwood, G.R., "Educational Research : Concepts and Models," *Journal of Educational Research*, Vol. XXI :2. June, 1995, pp. 71-82.

[31] Ibid.

# List of Readings

## Developing the Curriculum

**Behera, Santosh.** "Improving Professional Determination – Teacher as Researcher," *University News*. 36:45, (Nov 9, 1998). pp. 12, 13.

**Bhattacharya, G.C.** "Cafetaria Types of Courses in Teachers Education", *University News*, 41:18, (May 8–11, 2003). pp.6,7, & 8.

**Cornelius, D.J.K.** "The Tyranny of Examinations", Education Page, *The Hindu*, (June 22, 1999)

**Erth, Donald R.** "Education and National Development," Talk on Multidisciplinary Approach in Higher Education, *University News*, (June 12, 1989). pp.4–7.

**Goel, D.R., Chhaya Goel and Prerana Shelat.** "Transparency in Higher Education Evaluation." *University News*, 41:38. (Sept 22-28, 2003).

**Guha, A.S.** "Total Learning Situation – Learner Autonomy and Learner Contiguity," *University News*, 36:36, (Sept 7, 1998). pp.9,10.

**Kishore Das, Manvendra.** "Training Higher Education's Students and Teachers", *University News*, 37:17, (April 26, 1999), pp.3-6.

**Madhumita Bandopadhyaya.** "Quality Control of Doctoral Research: Role of Research Fellowships." *University News*, 41:29 (July 21-27, 2003).

**Mishra, S.B.S and P.K. Chatley.** "Self-evaluation System cum Delinking of Regress from Jobs," *University News*, (Nov.6, 1989).

**Pankaj, Ashok.** "Regulating Higher Education in India: Case for a Positive Role of the State," *University News*, 39:30, (July 23,2001). pp.7–12.

**Passi, B.R.** "Action Research for Staff Development," *University News*, 39:12, (March 19, 2001). pp.1–4.

**Pethe, Abbey.** "Increasing the Effectiveness of Teacher Training: a Fresh Look at Refresher Courses for College Teachers", *University. News*, 36:39, (Sept.28,1998) pp. 8–10.

**Rastogi, Savita.** "Academic Staff Development in Higher Education", *University News*, 37:8, (Feb.22,1999). pp. 2–6.

**Sanjay L. Mahajan.** "Whither our Research Priorities in Teacher Education", *University News*, 41:21, (May 26, 2003).

**Singh, Major and Ratoid, Harbans Singh.** "Research and Teaching: Complementary to Each Other", *University News*, 37:44, (Oct.1999), pp. 9–12.

**Trivedi, R.S.** "Curriculum for Teacher Education", *University News*, (Aug.14, 1995), p. 10.

**University Grants Commission.** "Manual of Evaluation Procedures for Accreditation", Documentation on Objectives, Structure and Policies and Manual of Evaluation Procedure for Accreditation *Journal of Higher Education*, Vol.18-2, (Summer, 1995). pp.310-319.

**Venkata Reddy, K.** "Criteria of Academic Excellence", *University News*, (Oct 16, 1989)

**Vijaya Kumar, B.** "Regeneration of Quality Research in Higher Education: Ways Ahead", *University News* 41:41, (Oct. 13–19, 2003).

**Yadav, S.K.** "Research Perspective on Teacher Education", *University News*, 41:22.

# Implementing the Curriculum

In the earlier chapters, developing curriculum content for a programme of education was stated to be a primary step, in which the educational objectives and the means to reach the objectives should be identified. The sources for identifying the objectives of an educational programme and a useful approach to identifying the abilities such as knowledge, skill and value as important forms of learning were also discussed. Since learning occurred through learning experiences the elements of a learning situation that provided the needed learning experiences were described. The concept of evaluation of learning as an integral part of learning was discussed.

Besides the aspect of content, the aspect of organization in a curriculum was pointed out. The importance of organizing learning experiences so as to provide continuity, sequence and integration of the content, so that what was learned was retained and was operational, was also discussed. When both the content and the organization of the content are planned the curriculum needs to be made operational by planning its implementation. In the following pages the factors involved in implementing a curriculum plan are presented.

# Factors Involved in Implementing a Curriculum Plan

There are certain key procedures, processes and concepts that will help in effective implementation of a curriculum plan. For implementing a teacher education programme, the following preliminary preparations will lead to an effective programme. Teacher educators need to consider the socio-economic characteristics of the particular population of prospective teachers who enrol as students so that the programme of education can be organized with regard to their professional needs, abilities, aspirations and the societal demands they are likely to face. In drafting particularized programmes, the teacher educators should gather together or meet with experienced teachers, sociologists, educational psychologists, economists, experts in political and administrative matters, forming a curriculum planning committee. Such committees could help in building a socially relevant, educationally sound and scientifically up-to-date curriculum in teacher education.

Suggestions for features to consider in a scheme of teacher education programme were collected from a study of literature on teacher education published between 1990 and 2001 (appendix VII). Such studies will help in adding to the relevance and authenticity of a teacher education programme and hence needs to be conducted periodically by teacher educators to evaluate the teacher education programme.

A traditional, systematically organized curriculum content is usually not in the form it can be directly implemented. It needs to be organized on the basis of psychology and principles of learning such as continuity, sequence and horizontal and vertical integration of content promoting learning for retention and transfer. Hence, the content needs to be further refined. The objectives as initially presented may not be specific enough to be evaluated for attainment of the objectives. They may need to be further refined so that the objectives are attainable through learning experiences that can be provided and attainment of the objectives can be evaluated.

## 1.1 Providing Learning Experiences

After the above preparatory steps, the first step in implementing the programme is to select the learning experiences that will lead to acquiring the kinds of abilities, knowledge, skills and values involved in the objectives set up. For this purpose teaching-learning situations need to be planned. A teaching-learning situation, it has been noted earlier, is one of the five elements, the other four being the teacher, student, learning materials and learning experiences, required for learning to happen. Teaching-learning situations are set up for creating a suitable environment and for presenting the materials for providing learning experiences.

The teacher's effort is not complete by merely seeing that the elements of a learning situation are present. An interaction with these elements needs to be brought about by motivating the learner to react to these elements, get involved in the situation, experience curiosity and feel the challenge posed by the problems they perceive in reaching their objectives. Only such an interaction will provide learning experiences. The learners should therefore be motivated first to react to the learning materials, the teacher and the subject matter content in a conducive learning situation. Motivation is the key to activating a curriculum plan after learning experiences are selected.

Motivation depends upon interaction between the elements of the learning situation, and interaction implies communication in one or more or all forms. The communication process needs to be maintained for keeping the interaction going and for providing learning experiences. The responsibility of the teacher does not stop here but extends to monitoring the effectiveness of the learning experiences so that there is progress in learning towards the objectives. This task calls for managing the communication process, the interaction and the learning experiences effectively. Hence the management process also is involved in implementing the curriculum of an educational programme. All these above factors implied in implementation of a curriculum are taken up in more detail in the following pages.

# Section 2 Concept and Role of Motivation in the Teacher Education Programme

Teacher educators need to have an understanding of the dynamics of human motivation so that they can motivate the prospective teachers to participate wholeheartedly in the teacher education programme. What would motivate prospective teachers to take an intrinsic interest in their professional education? Perhaps, if they develop a sense of importance of education to social development, they may be motivated to pursue earnestly their professional education. They should also become aware of the key role of teachers in making education effective in promoting social development, which will make them aware of the worth of becoming effective teachers through the teacher education programme.

Generally, student teachers who are enrolled will be ready to 'go through' the teacher education programme, since their aim would be to get a certificate of pass for getting an appointment in a teacher's post or for improving their prospects of promotion and tenure. Such extraneous motivation has produced many unmotivated teachers who form a part of the teaching staff of colleges and universities in India.[1]

Effort needs to be made in teacher education programmes to develop intrinsic motivation for teaching, so that dedicated teachers could be expected as an outcome of teacher education programmes.

The manner in which the teacher educator sets up a learning situation and motivates the prospective college teacher will be a demonstration of how motivation to learn can be promoted for prospective teachers to follow in their turn.

Motivating students to learn is seen to be the greatest hurdle in higher education in India. Both teachers and students have no intrinsic motivation to get involved in the educational process according to articles in several newspapers, journals and studies on higher education in India. Motivating learners is an important skill in teacher competence for the development of which an understanding of the concept, the ingredient forces and the dynamics of motivation are necessary.

It is important that teacher educators become fully informed as to how motivation of student teachers can be brought about for taking an intrinsic interest in their education. Teacher educators need to have a clear grasp of some of the widely accepted theories on the psychological factors and behavioral aspects of motivation and be able to apply their knowledge in their teaching. Scholarship in the fundamentals of educational psychology should be required in the education of teacher educators as much as for their student teachers.

When teacher educators understand and appreciate the role of motivation in learning they can motivate their students. Motivation of student teachers will be a primary task in implementing a teacher education programme. Sine there are several theories of motivation regarding the concept, basis, mechanism and behavioral aspects of motivation, the mastery of the present day knowledge about motivation is a daunting task. However, the phenomenon of motivation and the variables related to it are briefly described, keeping to some prominent theories, an understanding of which is expected to be helpful in teaching student teachers.

## 2.1 Some Concepts and Theories of Motivation [2]

Two forms of 'drives' arising from inner stimuli and intense painful external stimuli motivate beings to act and reduce or eliminate the stimulation or excitation. This is the function of every instinct, defense, action or habit that makes a person become active. This is the response to the first question as to what makes a person become active.

The second question that the theory of motivation deals with is "Why does the organism or person act one way rather than any other?" One answer to this is: 'habit', which refers to modes of behavior fixated through too much gratification or frustration.

Changing of behavior, freeing it from fixation, is by motivation through punishment or homeostatic need of the desired behavior, and by reinforcing the changed behavior to fix it. However there is an optimal level of stimulus variation below which increasing stimulus is reinforcing, and beyond which decreasing stimulus is reinforcing, presenting a curvilinear principle of reinforcement. 'Stimulus variation' refers to the difference between the strength of the existing stimuli and that of new stimuli: punishment or homeostatic need, applied to change behavior.

Another motivation theory that 'all behavior is motivated' is challenged by several behavioral scientists. They quote examples of 'play' when comfort is provided, exploration by laboratory rats only when they are well fed, only well fed monkeys learning to un-assemble a puzzle, and the enthusiastic and repeated performances of emerging skills by babies, as all occurring without no other stimulation.

Out of primary physiological needs arise a host of secondary needs, motives and drives, such as 'social approval', 'need for achievement', 'affiliation' and 'security'. These are 'push' factors of motivation. There are also 'pull' factors of motivation such as goals and incentives, ego-involvement and perceived values. Psychologists mention as external stimulus drives, such as 'manipulatory', 'exploratory' and 'sensory deprivation'. The tendency to be inquisitive, to be playful or to gamble, to take interest in 'doing' a task are stated to be external stimuli that becomes a chief source of motivation.

Modern theories of motivation hold that the notion of physiological states as a source of motivation is exaggerated and assign a secondary position to such internal stimuli. Harlow pointed out that no experimental literature showed that internal drives as more basic than external motivating agendas, and concluded that 'learning efficiency is far better related to tensions in the brain than in the belly' ![3] Bugelski suggested that motivation may boil down to getting the student's attention[4], an idea partially supported by Wittrock's study on the affect of 'set' on motivation.[5]

On reaching adulthood, growth expansion needs such as need for achievement, power, creativity, self-actualization, broader orientation of one's role, serve as motives. Such growth expansion motives seem to determine the first half of adult years. Factors of development too bring about changes in motivation. Environmental stimulus and expectations also motivate. When social norms change social pressures, motivations too may change. Change in age as one grows up may create new expectations due to which , earlier motivations may change. But sameness or absence of stimulus kills curiosity and hence motivation too.[6]

According to Maslow's hierarchy of human needs[7] in the course of growth one set of needs require satisfaction at one time and another set of needs at another time, changing motivations.[8]

Critical periods in life such as time limits, concentration of all threats at one point in time, may influence motivational pattern. Motivation will also be extinguished by continuous frustration of needs, caused by change in social status, too many demands, physical decline and change, threat due to technological advancement, external disturbing social situations and 'locked-in' situations where no change is possible.[9] According to Festinger, discrepancy between belief about a situation and perception of that situation producing 'cognitive dissonance' serves as a source of motivation.[10] Many psychologists have studied the mechanism of motivation and the factors involved. A list of readings on this topic is included at he end of this chapter.

It is important that teacher educators become fully informed as to how motivation as a key factor in the learning process can be brought into play in learning situations in teacher education. It will be useful to study the extraneous interests of the prospective teachers that prompted them to enroll themselves in the teacher education programme on hand.[11] The extraneous interests of the prospective teachers need to be gradually superseded by intrinsic interest in the profession of teaching during the course of a teacher education programme.*

* An illustration of a plan of a motivational unit as a starting point in a teacher education program is given in Appendix IX.

# Communication Process in Teaching

The notes given below in this section have been summarized from the ideas of scholars in the aspect of communication in teaching and learning.[12]

For motivation of learning, interaction of the learner with the elements of a learning situation is necessary. Interaction involves basically a two-way communication, which may be of two types: verbal and nonverbal, between the elements of a learning situation, stimulated by the presence of objects or events and initiated and directed by the teacher. The teacher should, therefore, understand the nature of the process of communication and become an effective communicator.

Communication is a two-way process requiring a communicator, a message, the vehicle or means of expressing the message, that is, speech or visual display, a channel such as transmitters, audio-visual materials, telephones and microphones and a receiver who understands and responds. Effective communication depends on the way the message is presented, the 'treatment' of the message, and an environment that facilitates the conveyance of the message. It also requires the preparation of the audience to accept, interpret and respond to the message. Unless a response is made, the communication is not complete.

Mental and emotional readiness, and physical readiness seen in the attention given by the audience, are necessary for effective communication. Emotional upsets, anger, hatred, aversion, fear, inferiority complex, and diffidence are all factors that may create barriers to effective communication. In popular language, the teacher as a communicator should be on the same 'wavelength' as the learners, if they are to interact with the teacher. A 'communication gap' may exist due to these barriers of communication.

Accepting a message from a communicator also depends on the 'credibility' of the communicator. For successful communication the credibility of the communicator is important and should be maintained. Some prominent leaders involved in the Family Welfare Programs in India have been heard to jokingly say that they may have no credibility with the people, to speak of limiting the family as they themselves had large families! If a teacher frequently gives erroneous information on the subject that is taught, the teacher will lose credibility as a good source of information. If a teacher does not practice what she or he preaches, the teacher will lose credibility as a sound advisor.

Skill on the part of the communicator to use the channels of communication effectively, and to treat the message in the way it will be clear and memorable will affect the success of communication. Some physical factors like the tone and pitch of voice and clarity of speech will affect success in communication. Also, noise in the surroundings by passing buses, trains, cars or planes overhead, loudspeakers, television and radio broadcasts and loud music or slogan shouting in processions on the street are all distractors that hinder successful communication during learning hours in educational institutions. Teacher educators should understand the science of good communication and develop skill in effective communication to serve as a model for the prospective teachers.

# Management Process in Planning for Teaching and During Teaching

Teaching-learning experiences need to be organized for a group of learners mostly in a classroom situation. It becomes the responsibility of the teacher to provide adequate learning opportunities equitably distributed among learners, and to competently guide their learning. This becomes important as prospective teachers are usually a heterogeneous group in different stages of adulthood and with different work experience. This means that resources for teaching and learning are to be efficiently used.

The resources at the disposal of teachers and learners are generally as below:

a) Materials intended for interacting with, such as books, pictures, objects and settings;

b) Time at the disposal of learners and teachers;

c) Space and environment for setting up learning experiences;

d) The different learning abilities of students, their background knowledge, skills and values.

e) The scholarship and skills of the teacher; and

f) The community's human resources and institutional resources.

The teacher should ensure the adequacy and availability of all these resources and plan the educational programme utilizing these resources on a short or long-term basis. Utilization of these resources should be planned for carrying on effectively the teaching-learning processes such as motivating, communicating, interacting and experiencing.

There is also administration of evaluative procedures that need to be managed so that every individual is evaluated and the evaluation process becomes also a learning process for both the teacher and the learner in regard to the efficacy of the teaching-learning methods and materials. After every class session a teacher should retrospect on the management problems faced and likely alterative management plans to be tried out in future situations.

# Putting the Implementation Plan to Work The Teaching Process

Section 5

It should be recalled that the main aim of teacher education was stated to be development of potential professional competency of the prospective teachers as educators in colleges and universities. Accordingly, the process of curriculum development for the education of college teachers was considered and planning of the curriculum content was examined. This was followed by a consideration of the implementation of the curriculum in actual classroom sessions with student teachers.

The key factor in implementation of any educational programme was seen to be motivation of the entrants to the programme. An illustration of a motivating unit is appended to suggest how the concept of motivation can be operationalised. At this point it will be useful to consider that a programme of education implies that the curriculum will be put to work by teachers through their teaching. Effective teaching is, therefore, a crucial process that will make a teacher education programme successful. Effective teaching is the responsibility solely of the teacher as educator. Effective teaching depends on understanding the concept and nature of the teaching process and the ability of the teacher in applying this understanding in directing the teaching process. A concept of the teaching process may be arrived at by a system of two kinds of treatment: namely, a) a scientific treatment or a study of its technological aspects. This is done by making a survey of the elements and their relationships in the process, identified by educators from their experiences and thinking and also from the biological and social sciences. b) a philosophic treatment. This will involve the study of the philosophical and social foundations of education that will lead to identifying what teaching is and ought to be.[13] It will be useful for teacher educators to be also aware of some of the major aspects of the teaching process as reflected in the opinion of some reputed scholars, as listed below:

1. The concept of teaching grows out of our concept of learning'. Teaching is a process of guided interaction between the teacher and the student, and the materials of instruction.[14]
2. Teaching is 'communication or transmitting of experience,' creating and setting in action the mind of the pupil, arousing his 'self-activities' and 'directing' them.[15]
3. "Thus all teaching is communication."[16]
4. The teacher's distinctive role is to challenge the learner into learning, instill interests to create a bond of friendship and confidence, a feeling of togetherness. The teacher 'senses' the 'teachable moments' and also 'causes' them to happen.[17]
5. Teaching is a continuous round of 'decision making in problem situations.[18]
6. Teaching is an art of choice in unresolved and continuously developing situations.[19]

All these above descriptions of the teaching process and many others in educational literature point to certain elements involved and the relationships among them. The elements give structure and their relationships describe the function of the teaching process. There are differences of opinion among educators, social scientists and thinkers in general as to what the nature and role of the different elements are and ought to be.

Chiefly, there are two distinct points of view about the nature of teaching. One view is that it is an art based on certain principles of psychology and educational theory. The other point of view is that it as a more precisely planned method, the activity of the teacher following more closely a planned detailed prescription relative to pupil activity.

What teaching is and ought to be, though helped by a study of the philosophic and social foundations of education, 'must be a process of discovery' on the part of the teacher, since it will be 'presumptuous' to present anything as the final answer.[20]

The teaching act appears to be wide ranging in the intensity of effort, push, or pull, made by the teacher to initiate and sustain the educative process. Twenty-five terms that describe the teaching act can be identified from the literature; these can be listed in an order of increasing involvement of the teacher, implying increasing control and responsibility for initiating the learning activity. The involvement of the teacher is seen to range from mild effort and minimum control in relation to pupil effort, through the phase of effort by teacher equal to that of the pupil, towards highest effort and control of the teaching-learning situation with the minimum passive pupil activity.* The effort of the teacher should be to pass from the phase of highest control to the phase of least control. This is a hallmark of effective teaching.

The teaching process arises out of the activity of the teacher in creating a learning situation, motivating the learner, guiding the learning experiences, and evaluating the attainments of the selected objectives. There needs to be a continuous effort on the part of the teacher to make the teaching process an outcome of a cooperative approach with the learner in pursuing the objectives set up.

Following a cooperative effort is important in teacher education as the learners will be adults and will be better motivated in becoming competent teachers if teacher education sessions are treated as a joint adventures in exploring the challenging terrain of the educative process.

It may be that such teaching will have a multiplier effect since this cooperative spirit will be carried to classes at the lower echelons of the educational system.

There is an enormous amount of research and theoretical literature accumulated over the decades of the twentieth century by the United States, Britain and all the other countries of the West, though a beginning in educational research and literature is being made in India. All that could be done in this general text on teacher education was to give a glimpse of such vast treasure of

* See Chart showing the Possible Range of Teacher Involvement in the Teaching Process and the Consequent Pupil Involvement in Learning, p. 150.

knowledge available on teaching and education by presenting a list of readings on the subject. Apart from this, it does not appear profitable to give a more detailed or a more scholarly discourse on the teaching process in this text, because learning about effective teaching is not an one time effort but a continuous lifeong professional pursuit.

*The Possible Range of Teacher Involvement in the Teaching Process and the Consequent Pupil Involvement in Learning*

| *Teacher Involvement* | *The Teaching Act* | *Pupil Involvement* |
|---|---|---|
| Effort: mild<br>Control:minimum | Encouraging<br>Helping<br>Aiding<br>Guiding<br>Facilitating<br>Enabling | Effort: high<br>Independence: high<br>Self-activity |
| Effort:equal to that of the pupil | Planfully intervening<br>Cooperating<br>Collaborating<br>Together engaging | Effort: equal to the teacher's active responsive |
| Greater effort | Influencing<br>Inducing<br>Motivating<br>Stimulating<br>Challenging | Responsive |
| Indirect control, and presence of environment felt | Choosing experiences<br>Arranging situations<br>Setting the stage<br>Providing opportunities<br>Creating opportunities<br>Setting up close working | Responsive,<br>Sensitive,<br>Receptive |
| Increased control and effort | Developing<br>Accelerating<br>Transmitting<br>Applying a procedure | Decreasing self-activity,<br>Passive |

# Some Preparatory and Auxiliary Tasks for Teacher Educators for their Professional Development

Teacher educators need to constantly look for resources that help in teaching and learning. These include examining reference reading materials suitable for recommending as 'readings' for their students. Teacher educators need to accumulate records of their insights into educating teachers from their experience in preparing college teachers, acquire sufficient scholarship in the subject of Education, and have a sound philosophical basis for writing booklets and textbooks useful for college teachers in aspects of teaching and developing curricular units at the college level.

Teacher educators need to broaden their understanding of ground realities operating in our Indian educational system and in the society in which they live. Keeping in touch with ground realities will help teacher educators to continuously improve the relevance of their curriculum to their students. They should build sufficient rapport with the society around so that they can make use of talented, scholarly or skilled people in their neighborhood to enrich their classroom experiences by their participation.

Teacher educators should themselves be good resource persons for some special activity in which their special abilities or interests are given expression. These could be gardening, collecting informative samples of materials, craftwork, innovative cookery, dress-making, carpentry, furnishing, collecting pictures on particular themes or antique objects, painting and drawing, and many other activities that express their special abilities. Teacher educators of home scientists need to be active, innovative homemakers and teach by example.

Teacher educators need to consider the socioeconomic characteristics of the particular population of prospective teachers who are students. This should be done so that the programme of teacher education can be organized to meet the professional needs, abilities and aspirations of the students and the social demands the students are likely to face. In drafting particularized programmes, the teacher educators should gather together or meet with experienced teachers, sociologists, educational psychologists, economists and political experts and form curriculum planning committees. Such committees could help in building relevant, educationally sound and scientifically up-to-date curriculum in teacher education. Such an exercise is important especially for teacher educators of college teachers of home science.

Teacher educators need to gain wide general knowledge about the world around by constantly reading newspapers and journals of general interest. If teacher educators become vibrant participants in social organizations and professional associations of different interest groups, they can make their teaching relevant to their students and the society, widen their mental horizons, offer a role model to the youth, and be an influential member of the society they serve. Such teacher educators can be expected to prepare superior college teachers who in their turn can be expected to offer high quality education needed to build strong, healthy and progressive Indian citizens.

## References Cited


1 Kapur. J.P. "Why Are Our Teachers Alienated From Higher Education System", *University News*, 37:2 (Jan 11, 1 999).

2 1. (a) Woodruff, Asahel D., and (b) Wright. Herbert, E. "Motivational Theory and Educational Practice", (pp. 341–342) "How Psychology of Motivation is Related to Curriculum Development", (pp.349–356) in *Educational Psychology.* edited by A.P.Coladarci, New York : Holt, Rinehart and Winstion, 1955.

2. (a) De Cecco. J.P. (b) Harlow, M.F., Introduction (chapter 2) and "Mice, Monkeys, Men and Motivation. Chapter 2: "Motivation: Does Curiosity Kill the Cat?" in *Human Learning in the School* edited by J.P. De Cecco, New York : Holt, Rinehart and Winston 1063. pp.85–97.

3 Harlow, M.F. *Op.cit.*, p.92.

4 De Cecco, J.P. Introduction. Chapter 2, *Op.cit.*, pp.83,84

5 ———. Ibid., pp. 82, 83.

6 Kuhlen. Raymond J. "Motivational Change During the Adult Years," *Psychological Backgrounds of Adult Education*, Chicago, Illinois: Center for Study of Liberal Education for Adults, 1963. pp. 77–108

7 Klausmeier, H.J. Chapter 2: "Motivation," *Learning and Human Abilities.* New York: Harper and Brothers, 1961. p.323.

8 Kuhlen, *Op.cit.*, pp.78,79

9 ———. Ibid., pp.82–108

10 Festinger, L. *A Theory of Cognitive Dissonance*, Harper and Row, 1957.

11 Rana, Ansuya. "Professional Commitment..." (unpublished thesis), *Supra,* chapter IV

12 Leagans,J.P. *The Communication Process in Rural Development*, Cornell International Agricultural Development Bulletin 1, Ithaca, New York: College of Agriculture, Cornell University, 1963.

13 Gross, H.C., P.S. Wronsky and J.W. Hanson, (eds) *School and Society :Readings in the Social and Philosophical Foundations of Education.* Boston: D.C. Health and Co., 1962. p.3.

[14] Knowles, M.S. Informal Adult Education, New York: Associate Press, 1955. p.31.

[15] Gregory, J.M. *The Seven Laws of Teaching*. Chicago: The Pilgrim Press. 1917.

[16] Hovland, Carl J. "Research Frontiers in Human Relations," *Social Communication*, 1948.

[17] Lane and Beauchamp, *Human Relations in Teaching.*

[18] Simpson, *Improving Teaching-Learning Process.* New York: Longmans Green and Co., 1953. pp.6,7,20 and 34.

[19] Gross, et al. *Op.cit.*

[20] Ibid.

## List of Readings

**Altbach**. *The Decline of Guru: The Academic Profession in Developing and Middle-Income Countries,* New York: Palgrave Publishers, 2000.

**Arora, G.L.** *Teachers and Their Teaching:Need for New Perspectives*. Delhi: Ravi Books, 2002.

**Bhat, Surekha and K. Ramanarayanan,** "Compilation of a Teaching Portfolio," *University News,* 37:42, (Oct., 18, 1999), pp. 1,2.

**Blair, Glenn Meyers**, "How Learning Theory is Related to Curriculum Organisation," *Readings in Educational Psychology*, edited by Victor H Noll and Rachel Noll, New York: The Macmillan Company, pp.206–212. College

**Boulding, K.E.** *The Image*, Ann Arbour, Michigan: The University Michigan Press, 1956.

**Brown, J.W. and Thomton, J.N.** *Teaching: Perspectives and Guidelines*, New York: McGraw Hill Book Co., 1963.

**Brown, Judson S.** *The Motivation of Behaviour,* New York : McGraw Hill Book Co., Inc., 1961.

**Burner, Jerome S.** *The Process of Education*, New York: Random House Inc., 1963.

**Bugeloski, B.R.** *The Psychology of Learning* New York: Henry Holt and Co., 1956.

**Cantor, Nathniel**, *The Teaching-learning Process*, New York: The Dryden Press, 1963.

**Chhatre, P.K.** *Technique and Practice of Teaching* Baroda: East and West Book House, 1954.

**Clark-Sloan.** *Classrooms on the Main Streets,* New York: Teachers College Press, 1966.

**Cormack, M.L.** *She Who Rides the Peacock.:Indian Students and Social Change,* Bombay: Asia Publishing House, 1961.

**Deshpande, M.V.** "Quality and Administration of Higher Education Under Globalisation: Challenges and Remedies," *University News*, (March 10–16), 2003.

**Ganchi, D.A.** "A New Paradigan for Educational Management in 21st Century," *Univcrsity News*, 38:17, (April,24, 2000), pp.1–4.

**Henderson, Norman, K.** *University Teaching*, Hong Kong University Press Oxford University Press, Madras.

**Highest, Gilbert,** *The Art of Teaching,* New York: Alfred Knopf, 1950.

**Hunt, H.C.** *Becoming an Educator,* Boston: Houghton-Mifflin Company , 1063.

**Hunter, Madeline**, *Motivation Theory for Teachers*. Calif: Corwin Press, 1986. Review by R.P. Singh, Jl. of Ed. Planning and Adm'n, Vol XIII: 4 (Oct., 1999). p. 493.

**Kamat, A.R.** "Education and Social Change: A Conceptual Framework," *Higher Education in India: The Social Context*, edited by Amrik Singh and G.D. Sharma, Delhi: Konark Publishers, 1989.

**Kudva, Pramila,** "Professional Aspects and Teacher Burn-out: A Relationship," *University News*, 38:7, (Feb., 14, 2000). pp.13–17.

**Kumar, Rajesh and Birendra Kumar**, "Immediacy Behaviors of University Teachers- A study," *University News*. 3 7:3 9, (Sept. 27,1999). pp.8.10.

**Manvendra, Kishore Das,** "Training Higher Education Students and Teachers: Abercrombie Approach," *University News* 37:17, (April 26,1999). pp.3-6.

**Mohanty, Sunil Behari**, "Effective Classroom Management in Higher Education," *University News*, 49, (Dec.4,1989). pp. 6, 9, 11.

——— "Effective Teaching in Colleges," *University News*, Vol.40, (Oct.2,1989). pp.43–51.

**Moore, W.E.** *The Professions: Roles and Rules*. New York: Russel Sage, 1970.

**Paintal, Iris**, *Micro-teaching: A Handbook for Teachers.* Delhi: Oxford University Press. 1980.

**Panton, J.H.** *Modem Teaching Practice and Techniques,* Longmans Green and Co., 1948.

**Pasis, B.K.** Microteaching in Teacher Education. Baroda: Center for Advanced Study in Education, M.S. University, Baroda.1974.

**Passi, B.K.** "Mass Higher Education – But With a Difference", *University News*, 38:39,2001, pp.13–7.

———. "Educational Management Through DBMS, *University News*, (June 29,1992).,11$69.

**Pressey, S.L. and** *Psychological Development Through Life Span.* New York: Harper, 1987.

**Ranga Sai, C.V.S.** "Developing Quality Management Systems in Higher education: Current Perspectives," *University News*, (March 10–16,2003).

**Rathore, N.C.S.** "Participatory Decision-making in the Management of Higher Education," *University News*, 41:48, (Dec. 1-7, 2003).

**Raya Prabhakaran,** "Teachers Associations-Some Views," Education: Open Page, The Hindu. (Nov.22, 1994).

**Seetharaman, R.** *Becoming a Better Teacher*, Chennai: University of Madras, Academic Staff College.

**Takur, C.P.** "Human Dimensions of Change," Review of Management of Change Through Human Resource Development by Maheshwar, B.L. and Dharu, P. (New Delhi: Tata Mcgraw Hill Pvt. Ltd. Co., 1991), *University News* (June 29, 1992).

# Postscript

In conclusion, as the author of this text I wish to reiterate that my intention was to provide a fairly readable text dealing with the essential concepts and understandings for becoming an effective teacher educator. A regrettable fact of the present times in India is that a majority of entrants to the teaching profession do not join education courses out of enthusiasm or conviction for the subject, but opt for education due to lack of opportunity to join other courses or find employment in other walks of life than that of a teacher. Consequently, teachers in general are not enthusiastic in making any voluntary effort to read educational literature and are easily put off any serious non-fictional literature. It is against this background that a text on Education and Teaching was to be made easy to read and understand, and the effort of the author has been towards this end.

I am also aware that at present there is no requirement for an education degree or even university credits to be earned in a teacher education course to be eligible for teaching in colleges and university departments. Hence there may be a very few university departments of education offering courses for those who opt to become college or university teachers. This means that there is no established body of teacher educators, that can be the target of a text for preparing college teachers.

However there are recent indications of an emerging demand for an established regular scheme of education for preparing college and university teaching as educators giving rise to the need for preparing teacher educators too, who can teach Education as a subject. One hopes that this demand materializes in the near future and departments of education will be started as an integral part of the mainstream of the university educational system. Only after the subject of Education is introduced as an important social science on par with sociology, psychology and economics, it will be feasible to require teachers in service or graduates as prospective college teachers to study the subject of Education as a prerequisite to employment in colleges and universities. The present patchwork scheme of conducting university eligibility tests nationwide would also become redundant.

It is the hope of the author that general information as to the essentials of the educative process, the extensive reading lists, and the classified summary of educational issues and objectives as perceived by Indian scholars in the field of Education, and other references in the appendices will induce teacher educators to read further. Educators preparing competent college and university teachers are expected to serve as the fountainhead of high quality university education in India.

# Appendices

## Appendix-I

### Chapter Two

### Notes on "A Modern Approach to the Development of Educational Philosophy"*

The process of developing educational philosophy, says Brubacher, starts with the 'humble data of common sense' and gathers into this bag data from science and history, paying special attention to life sciences of biology and psychology, and the social sciences of sociology, politics, and economics, as well as educational history. The data of morals and religion too should be added.

To achieve a philosophic synthesis all these above data are submitted to three methods of synthesizing : namely, speculative, normative, and critical, and it is the critical analysis of these data, explains Brubacher, their normative connotations and speculative theories they support, with which philosophy does its characteristic work.[1]

Brubacher refers to four major philosophical questions from a study of which emerged three disciplines of philosophy. The questions as to what are the generic traits of existence and what is the nature of human nature gave rise to Metaphysics: the theory of being or reality. From the, question as to what is reality, truth or

* Extracts from *Modern Philosophies of Education* by Brubacher, *Op.cit.*

knowledge, arose the discipline of Epistemology: the theory of knowledge. The question of what is the nature of value is dealt with by the discipline of Ethics: the theory of values.[2]

Each of these philosophical questions evoked more than one kind of response so that there are several life philosophies and consequently several educational philosophies. Specific questions related to each major philosophic question need to be asked for developing an education philosophy as a basis for educational decisions and as guidelines for educational practices. These questions and their educational implications as discussed by Brubacher,are presented below.

1. Should change, novelty, and time be taken as generic traits of nature, or as merely appearances of reality?

   Consequently, is education a process of unfolding what was primordially enfolded, and so should steer its course only by looking for challenges, primordial, and eternal? Should education accept a supernatural force as the prime mover of nature?

   Or, alternatively, should educational process treat change, novelty, and time as traits found in nature and give importance to natural order? [3]

2. Is human nature relatively constant in the midst of changes in the world around, or is it subject to a field of forces, requiring continued adjustment and modification? [4]

3. Is truth or knowledge (a) a precise correspondence of the knowable with the known, or (b) sensory and mental reactions to reality and found in the consistency of our constructs of reality, or (c) is it that which leads to a successful adaptation to environment – that which works?[5]

4. Are values subjective in the mind of man, or objective, intrinsic and found in the object?[6]

The various points of view in response to these questions give rise to many educational philosophies.

In addition, there are also those points of view, which arise in relation to education in different social, political, and economic settings. In the context of these settings, there are social philosophies described as autocratic, oligarchic, or democratic, grouped into two categories. One, that stresses the individual, and the other, the group, as more important.[7] Depending on the political setting and the social philosophy holding sway, there are in general two major philosophies of education: the totalitarian and the pluralistic. Underlying the latter there are two attitudes toward education: the laissez faire and the positive.[8]

Likewise, one economic system will provide liberal education as a privilege of the economically capable, while another economic system will provide universal education for all, making both cultural and vocational studies widely available.[9]

Educational philosophies differ also with respect to several convictions born of educational practices and experiences in the educational process, such as whether a school should be progressive or conservative, what teaching strategy should be followed and what the professional obligations of the teacher are.[10] Then there are religious and moral schools with philosophies of secularism, humanism and theology, each with a different educational philosophy.[11]

Though these educational philosophies generally differ from one another, they also overlap in a few aspects. Attempts have been made to evolve a consensus among educational philosophers as to an overall educational philosophy in the educational system of a country, and eminent educators like Brubacher have stressed that consensus is necessary for a society to be cohesive.[12]

# Appendix-II

## Historical Sources of Life Philosophies of India

Very ancient roots of life philosophy in India can be traced back to the earliest human settlements in the Indus valley from about 3000 B.C., when mud and mud-brick dwellings, increasing variety of kitchen utensils and craft tools along with wheel-thrown pottery came into existence. From archeological evidence one can gather that an urge for better materials, cleanliness, appreciation of beauty, and respect for a 'mother goddess' became the motivating forces or values in the human groups of this age.

There has been continuity of cultural characteristics and development of distinct settlement patterns and a wide range of pottery decorations throughout the following millennium leading to the new Harappan culture.[13] In the Indus valley basin, during the closing centuries of the third millennium, there was a rapid development of agriculture, cattle raising, and building of admirably planned townships built with burnt bricks to withstand the flooding of rivers. Honesty in trade was ensured by instituting a system of uniform weights and measures.[14]

Evidences of what is described as an 'explosion' in civilization is found in Mohenjo-daro, Harappa and many other 'Harappan culture' centers, extending to the Ganges basin to the east, and Cambay to the south. Such development could have been achieved only by a disciplined cooperative society based on moral values of concern for the community welfare, as seen in the drainage system, the granaries and the public baths for which the Harappan culture is famous.[15]

The people of the pre-Harappan and Harappan civilisations who were supposed to be Dravidians were, presumably, pushed gradually to the east and the south after about 1750 B.C. by the Aryan immigrant groups of the Vedic culture.[16] The theory of Aryan invasion is strongly refuted by a later writer[17], but is subject to an ongoing controversy.

However, the early cultural-values and practices appear to have co-existed with the newer waves of cultural beliefs and practices or were partly absorbed to form a composite culture that both changed with the times and also showed continuity from the pre-Harappan to the present age.[18] Still, nothing conclusive could be said about the history of the post-Harappan and Vedic ages, except that abundant debates and research by archaeologists, linguists, and historians are being carried on at present.

Alongside of the Vedic system of religion, from early times non-Vedic systems of religious beliefs like Natha, Yoga, and Siddhacara cults too widely prevailed in India and claimed to find all the religious mysteries in the human body itself. They included the mysteries of the human body such as solar and lunar currents within the nervous system and the psychic centers of the body. The yogis produced considerable studies in physiology and medicine and introduced the yoga system of exercises. The tantrics produced the Samnhitas or Agarnas, consisting of knowledge, yoga, kriyu (practices) and carya (conduct). The tantrics worshipped Siva-Sakti and the mother goddess, were liberal in social and caste restrictions, and did not perceive women as inferior in status.[19]

Other early sources of life philosophies are the epics: Ramayana, Mahabharata and other puranas, especially, the Vishnu Purana and the Bhagavatham that were orally composed and developed during the first millennium B.C. and reached their final form,between the fourth and second century B.C. The chief actors in these epics, like Rama and Krishna, rise to divine heights by their noble deeds and are regarded as avatars of the Supreme Being and have been the source of philosophical guidance to the people. While speculative theories as to the nature of existence, reality, and the universe form one aspect of the Hindu religion, another aspect is its moral code of conduct about what men ought to do according to the religious concept of the universe. The epics too contributed to the formation of a moral code of conduct upheld by many generations of Indians up to the present.[20] An important part of Hindu philosophy are six systems of philosophy known as the

Sutras, developed by 200 A.D., after the climax reached by Buddhism and Jainism, though their beginnings may have been as early as 800 B.C., and they dealt with questions on the nature of thc world, sources of knowledge, evolution of life and the process of self-realization. Of these six systems, the Nyaya school, using logical methods, recognizes four sources of knowledge: perception (pratyaksha), inference (anumana), analogy (upamana), and credible testimony (sabda); and the principle of causation and analysis of the process of reasoning.[21a]

In the Vaiseshika school's cosmology, all material objects are combinations of four kinds of 'atoms' earth, water, fire and air, and nine non-material substances such as space, time, ether, mind and soul. According to the Samkhya school the universe is composed of two entities of consciousness: Pursha and Prakriti, which influence all material and physical resources of nature and evolve the world. Prakriti has three conflicting aspects: Sattva (light, purity and harmony ), Rajas (energy, passion), and Tamas (inertia, darkness). Evolution proceeds through the development of 'buddhi', then self-sense, feeling of ego, and then gradually the five cognitive organs, five motor organs, and a disciplined mind. Knowledge of distinction between purusha and prakriti (self and non-self) gives emancipation.[21b]

The yoga school believed that an omnipotent and omniscient God controlled the process of evolution, and, not only knowledge but also discipline of mind and body is needed for emancipation. About 400 B.C. Jaimini wrote the purva-mimamsa, the fifth school of philosophy, interpreting the Vedas and inquiring into the nature of 'Dharma' (right action). After this came the sixth school of philosophy, the 'Vedanta' system of philosophy, beginning with the writing of the Brahma sutra by Badravana. Along with the Brahma sutra, the Upanishads and the Bhagavad Gita formed the foundation of the Vedanta school.[21c]

Of the Vedanta school there are two main categories: one is the 'Advaita' school of which the most famous exponent is Samkara in the eighth century A.D., who said that the world was neither real nor quite unreal but an appearance, a manifestation of the Brahman. Samkara explains with an analogy. "A person may mistake a rope for a serpent. The serpent is not there, but it is not entirely an illusion, for there is a rope. The appearance of the serpent lasts until the rope is closely examined. The world can be compared with the serpent and Brahman with the rope".[21d] A predecessor to Samkara was an extreme monist, Gandapada, for whom the external world was unreal, a vast illusion and nothing existed other than the Brahman. Like the Buddhist spiritual absolutist Nagarjuna, he denied 'the possibility of change or the validity of causation'.

The second category of the Vedanta school was the school of 'Dvaita' philosophy of Ramanuja and Madhva, in the eleventh and thirteenth centuries respectively. Ramanuja claimed that the individual souls and the concrete world were like the body of God, distinct but not separate from God (Isvara) and Isvara, possessed of both, is the Brahman. Though all were within Brahman, individual souls were different from Isvara. This approach helped the intellectual acceptance of the 'Bhakti' movement of approaching God through devotion rather than through knowledge'. Madhva believed that the individual souls were separate from Brahman, and that the world was real, but Brahman was the highest reality, complete and perfect.[21e]

## The Bhakti Movements

It can be said that the substratum of religious and philosophical literature of India is chiefly of loving devotion to a chosen God, having roots in Dravidian culture of worship of the image of a mother goddess of fertility, of Shiva, the phallus or the *lingham,* of holy trees like the *Pipal* and of the rivers *thirthas.* The undercurrent of loving devotion focused on human incarnations (*avatars*) of God swelled into bhakti movements from time to time beginning even earlier to the time Krishna was worshipped.[22]

"Besides anthropomorphic Gods, the pre-Aryan people had many animistic and totemistic gods. Tribal mingling led also to the mingling of the gods. Thus, much popular religion of pre-Aryan origin got mixed up in the elaborate Aryan rituals as well as in their domestic rituals. This line of development paved the way to growth of popular Hindusim".[23]

Between 200 B.C. and A.D. 300 there were two schools following the 'bhagawati' or the bhakti' cult that exalted the path of devotion. One was the Bhakti school of Vaishnavism that worshipped Vasudeva-Krishna. The other was Siva bhagavatis who practiced Saivism.[24]

The predominantly Dravidian culture of the South produced scholars and philosophers who were another source of the life philosophies of India. The most ancient language of the South is Tamil. The Tamil compilation of the counsels of wisdom and morals in many aspects of life, known as *Thirukural*, composed sometime about 470 A.D. forms a major source of the life philosophy of the Tamils of South India.[25] The Kural has two-line verses that extol that kind of learning which is thorough and which delves deeply into the meaning of whatever is studied and exhorts practicing that which was learned. It stresses the enduring and indestructible value of Education and describes true learning as that which creates a thirst for more learning. The Kural holds that extension of education to others is a social imperative for the educated person.[26]

There are also many other scholar-poet- philosophers whose devotional writings and sayings are of great merit and antiquity, not only in Tamil but also in all the other languages of the Deccan. "Broadly stated. till about the close of the sixth century A.D. different religious sects lived together in admirable harmony".[27a] Between the 'dark period' before A.D. 550 and tenth centuries A.D. in the South, there were twelve Vaishnavite Tamil saint poets called *Alwars,* of whom one was a woman named Andal, sixty three Nayanmars, who were saivite saint poets of whom one was Karaikal Ammai, a woman.[27b] Between fourteenth and seventeenth century A.D. in the north there were saint poets, namely, Meerabai, Namadeva, Tukaram, Vallabhacharya.

Vilvamangala, Caitanya, Jayadeva, Vidyapati, Chafdidasa, Samkaradeva, most of whom were in Vishnu bhakti movement.[28a]

Many of the bhakti saints were of low castes and all decried the caste system. They gave rise to both purely devotional and scholarly literature couched in the popular languages of their regions enriching the value systems which rejected ritualistic ceremonies and image worship, The Sivakavya of the seventeenth century A.D.' Somanada and Abhinava Gupta of Kashmir in the eleventh century A.D. and the Lingayats of Karnataka in the twelth century A.D. nurtured schools of philosophy that stressed devotion and faith. From the pre-Aryan days came the worshippers of the mother goddess as Shakti, called the Saktas, whose movement later connected with Tantrics. Shakti is worshipped in the form of Kali or Durga even today.[28b]

Between the twelfth and the seventeenth centuries the establishment of the Muslim rule brought in the Muslim patterns of culture in which also arose the devotional tradition of Islamic **Sufis.** The bhakti movements and Islamic Sufism existed side by side, influencing each other. The first Sufi teacher in 1193 A.D. was Kwaja Minuddin Cishti whose 'dargha' in Ajmer is famous for its Muslim and Hindu disciples. Between 1370 A.D. and 1440 A.D. lived Ramanada who gave 'medieval mysticism' its momentum by challenging caste divisions, traditional religious ceremonies, 'and accepted only the Hindu philosophy of knowledge, meditation (yoga) and devotion (bhakti) as the enlightened path in life'. Ramanada's followers were Kabir–a weaver, Ravidas–a cobbler, and Dadu–a cotton carder, who combined both sufism and bhakti faiths and preached in the language of the common people.[29]

Dadu founded the Brahma Sampradya without rituals and stated that the essence of the Brahma society was 'giving up self-regard, the worship of God, curing all corruptions of the mind and body, and cultivation of friendliness for all creatures', Dadu's famous follower, Rajjab, said: 'All this world is the Vedas, and the entire creation is the Koran" and "the worship of different sects, which are like so many small streams, move together to meet Hari (God) who is like the ocean."[30]

Of the sixteenth century mystics, Tulsidas and Dharmadas looked upon God as 'loving and intensely lovable creator, and in the seventeenth century, the Sufi Biru Sahed was a Hindu who had a Muslim disciple, Yera Shah,' who called upon both Allah and Rama or Hari in his devotional songs'. In Sind also there were mystic saints, and in Bengal emerged the Bauls, 'the most moving example of the simple(sahaj) man's search for the 'Man of my heart', whose religious tradition grew upon the ruins of Buddhism, Tantra, and Vaishnavism. The *Bauls* came from the lowest strata of Hindu and Muslim folds, sought 'freedom from all outward compulsions', 'accepted no divisions of society such as caste or class, no special deity, nor temple or mosque,' but were ascetics, believing that earthly love helps to find Divine love. They believed in harmony between the past, present, and future, and in harmony between material and spiritual needs. Though they had 'gurus' they held all experience to be their gurus and did not depend on any particular guru.[31]

The bhakti movement used poetry and music as its medium of its devotional and philosophic messages couched chiefly in the languages of the common people. Such great saints as Tulsidas, Ravidas, Kabir, Tukaram, Surdas. and Mirabai composed verses and sang with their followers, moving around the countryside building up the tradition of the 'bhajan' in the streets, temples, and 'mandaps'.

Another group of saintly scholars composed more complex, refined, devotional songs in the language of the region in which they lived. Some of these great composers and musicians were Thvagaraja. Syama Sastri. Muthuswany Dikshitar, Naravana Thirthar, Sadasiva Brahmam, Jayadevar. Purandaradas. Bhadrachala Ramadas, Swati Thirunal, Annamacharya, all who laid the foundation of devotional classic music. This list is not exhaustive as there has been a great galaxy of devotees and mystic poets in all the religions who have bestowed to the people prayers to give tranquility of mind, generate love of creation, a sense of sharing with others the joys and sorrows of life, of unity of religious goals amidst diversity of religious practices.

In the early eighth century A.D. many Zoarastrians from Persia fled by sea and by coastal route to western India to escape religious persecution by Arab armies, and given asylum by the Chalukyas, and settled as traders. They became the founders of the Parsi community[32], which is in course of time added prosperity to India and their religious philosophy of life. Zoarastrianism emphasized awareness of the Good and evil Forces, of the struggle of the good spirit against the evil ones, and of the need for self-discipline. Belief in the ultimate triumph of good over evil, value for uprightness in action, and value for the welfare of human and animal life were reflected in the philosophy of education upheld by Parsis.[33]

With regard to the impact of the religious philosophy of Islam on the life philosophies of people and on the earlier educational philosophers of India, it "did not lead to any marked change in the educational thought or practice of the country", but there was a change from the religious to a secular bias especially during the reign of Akbar, in giving equal opportunities to members of all communities, importance to practical arts and in directing education of a child to follow the child's interest and understanding, rather than the traditional method of learning the alphabet and reciting from books.[34]

Islam preached brotherhood, concern for the poor, and value for truth, humility, honesty, chastity, abstinence and justice. Christianity, through the Ten Commandments, stressed the same values and gave importance to Christ's preaching of the power of love over brute force. Jesus Christ through parables and exemplary acts of compassion spread the message of love, sacrifice and the spirit of service of mankind.

The interaction of Muslim and Hindu cultures produced a synthesis of the core values of the religions in bhakti movements as 'Sufism' and 'Sikhism'. In the fifteenth century A.D. Guru Nanak, a disciple of Kabir, founded Sikhism through his teachings, By the sixteenth century, Arjun, the fifth guru, established the Adi Granth, the holy scripture of the Sikhs, in which both the religious rituals and worship of idols by Hindus, and the religious observances and worship at Mecca by Muslims were rejected. Sikhism does not recognize caste or creed distinctions, stands for freedom of women and their equality with men. The Granth Sahib sets forth, "the purity of life as the highest object of human endeavour', and that loyalty, chastity, honesty, justice, mercy, and temperance are among the virtues on which vital stress is laid". Guru Nanak wherever he went proclaimed that 'there was but one God', under whatever name He was worshipped or remembered, and that 'He is best worshipped in selfless of humanity."[35]

The Jews too found a place of refuge in India and followed Judaism in the synagogues they established, chiefly along the western coastal areas of India. It is not known whether the Jewish religious philosophy influenced people but there was no hostility towards Jews due to prevalence of religious tolerance in the country.

# Appendix-III

## Bibliography of Publications from which Statements Reflecting Educational Philosophy and Areas of Concern were Identified and Classified Under Different Aspects of Education*

**Ambirajan,S.** "The Tragedy of Higher Education," *The Hindu*, April,7,1999.

**Behera, Santosh.** "Improving Professional Determinants - Teacher as a Researcher," *University News* (Nov.9, 1998) pp. 12,13,

**Bhat, Vignesh.** "Higher Education for 21st Century – a Cultural Reflection," *University News* (August, 2. 1999).

**Brubacher, J.** "The school and Social Progress," *Modern Philosophies of Education*, pp.230, 270.

**Bruner, J.S.** *The Process of Education*, Massachusettes: Harvard University Press.1962.

**Chalant, K.S.** "The Changing Scenario of Higher Education: Coping with the Challenges of the Twentieth Century," *University News* Vol. 41:28 (July 14–20, 2003), pp.2,3.

**Chatterjee, T.K.** "Crisis in Higher Education – Nature and Sources," *University News* (Jan. 25,1999), pp.1–8.

**Chaudhary, Uma Rao Singh.** "Restructuring Teacher Education – Need for Paradigm Shift," *University News* (May 17, 1999), pp.1–7.

**Chauhan, C.P.S.** "An Innovative Look at Teacher Education," *University News* (Oct. 1999). pp.10.11.

**Choudhary, S.C.** "State of Bihar Universities: Why This Decline?" *The Hindu* (October 9,1990).

**Chidambaram, R.** "Pursuit of Excellence," Convocation Address, *University News* (April 21, 1997).

* Appendix IV: Areas of Concern in between 1990 and 2001.

**Clement, A.** "Humanistic Education," *The Hindu* (1995).

**Das, B.C.** "Indian Society and Education in the Twenty First Century," *University News* (June 23, 1999). pp. 9-13.

**Correa, Charles.** "The Philosophy of Life," Convocation Address, *University News* (Nov., 25,1996).

**Deshmukh, K.G.** "Universities and higher Education in the 21st Century" *University News* (July, 13,1998). pp.4–6.

**Desi, Avtar.** "His her Education and Development Strategy," *University News* (July, 18,1994). pp.5–6.

**Dube, S.C.** "Higher Education and Social Change," *Higher Education In India: The Social Context*, (eds) Amrik Singh and G.D. Sharma, New Delhi: Konark Publishers Pvt.Ltd., 1988.

**Dutta, P.K.** "Relevance of Indian Education in Contemporary Indian Society," *University News,* Vol. 41:32, (August 11–17), 2003.

**Editorial.** *Business World* (Sep. 2–15,1991), p.37.

**Ghanchi, D.A.** "Academic Freedom: The Fractious Scenario of Indian Higher Education," *University News* (Sept. 23,1996), pp. 5–11.

**———.** "Higher Education : Constraints and Strains," *University News*, (Jan.4,1993), pp.5–11.

**———.** "New Directions of Teaching at Higher Level,"

**———.** "Three Myths of Indian Higher Education," *University News*, Vol.27:6,(Nov.6,1989).pp. 1–5.

**George, Raju.** "Catalysts of Social Change," *The Hindu* (Aug.27, 1996), pp.116–121.

**Gaurihar, Noorjahan N. and Shoba S Nilavar,** "The Need for Professionalisation in Teacher Education, *University News* (Dec.20, 1999), pp.1–5.

**Gopalan, K.** "Higher Education in India: Problems and Perspectives," *University News* (Jan. 9, 1995), pp.1–10.

**Government of India.** "Revamping Teacher Education," extracts from Chapterl: The Context: "Curriculum Framework for Teacher education," National Policy on Education, 1986, *University News* (Nov.25, 1996) pp.29–36.

**Guha, S.** "Total Learning Situation – Learner Autonomy and Learner Contiguity," *University News* (Sep.7, 1998), pp. 9,10.

**Hariharan, Meena.** "Measuring Professional Competence – New Evidences," *University News* (March 29,1999), pp.14,15.

**The Hindu Sub-editorial.** "A Major Challenge," *The Hindu* (June, 29, 1991).

**Hopper, W.A.E.** "Exploring Avenues to Study and Employment Education," *The Hindu* (July 22, 1997).

**Hussain, Zakir et al.** "Education and Traditional Values: A Symposium," *The Education Quarterly* Vol. XV: 50 (June, 1963).

**Jharta, H. and B. Jharta.** "Education System in India: Problems and Perspectives," *University News* (June 5, 1995) pp. 9–12.

**Kabir, Hunnayun.** *Indian Philosophy of Education*, New Delhi: Asia Publishing House, 1964.

**Kamat, A.R.** "Education and Social Change: A Conceptual Framework," *Higher Education in India*: The Social Context, (eds.) Amrik Singh and G.D, Sharma, New Delhi: Konark Publishers Pvt. Ltd., 1988. pp.25–45.

**Kapur, J.N.** "Why Are Our Teachers Alienated From the Higher Educational System?" *University News*, Vol. 37:2 (Jan. 11, 1999).

**Kasturirangan,K.** "Education as Liberators," Annual Convocation Address at University of Burdwan, *University News*, (May 24, 1999), pp. 13–16.

**Krishnaiyer, V.R.** "Priorities in Education," Convocation Address at Kolhapur University, Shivaji University (April 22,1996), pp.12–17.

**Kulandaiswamy, V.C.** "Higher Education Leads Towards Leadership," *University News* Vol.31:39, (Sep. 29, 1999), pp.13–16.

**Mahcswari.** "An Alternative Agenda for Higher education," *University News* (Oct.1, 1998), pp.1,2.

**Management Supplement.** "Management Self-learning in Training Programmes," *The Hindu* (Jan. 4, 1990), p.18.

**Marmar Mukhopadhyaya.** "Recruitment is the Key to Quality Education." *The Hindu* (July.1990).

**———.** "Taxonomy of Education," *University News* (June 28, 1999), pp.1–4.

**Mehrora. R.C.** "Professional Development of Teachers Orientation Programmes and Refresher Courses," *University News* (Jan. 4, 1993), pp.6–

**Menon P.N. and Sunil Dull.** Work Ethos and Faculty Accountability," *University News* , (Sep. 3).1996). pp.6–8.

**Mohanty, Sunil Behari.** "Excellence of Training teachers in Higher Education," *University News* (Sep.8, 1997).

**———.** "Education as an Investment," *University News* Vol.37:37. (Sep. 13. 1999), pp.1–5.

**Naik, K.R.** "Education and Socio-economic Development," *University News* (June 14, 1993), pp.1,2.

**Nanda, Renu.** "Radhakrishnan's Reflections on Education," *University News* Vol.4 1: 19, (May 12–18, 2003), p.16.

**Nath, K.P.** "Education and Socio-economic Development," *University News*, (May 12–18, 2003), p.16.

**Pandey, Saroj.** "Road Map to Quality INSET Need Based Training," *University News* (July 5, 1999).

**Prabhakran, R.** "Teachers Associations – Some Views," Education, *The Hindu* (Nov. 22, 1994), p.26.

**Prakash, Om.** "Relevance of Education," *University News* (Aug. 10, 198), pp.1–3.

**Prasad Rao, C.R.** "Higher Education in India," Review article of *Higher Education in India: the Social Context* (eds,) Amrik Singh and G.D. Sharma. *University News.* 1989.

**Pyle, M.V.** The Challenge of 21st Century." *University News* (Sep. 8,1997), pp. 16–22.

**Ramachandran Nair, R.** "History, Economics and Sociology of Higher Education in India, *University News*, (March 21, 1994), pp.3.

**Rao, Sudlha K.** Convocation Address at the Annual Convocation of the DAV College For Women, Amritsar, *University News*, Vol. 37:2 (Jan. 11, 1999)

**Rastogi, Savitha.** "Academic Self-development in Higher Education," *University News*, (Feb. 22, 1999), pp.2–6.

**Reddy, K.V.** "Criteria of Academic Excellence," *University News*, (Oct. 16, 1989), pp.3, 4.

**Ruhela, S.P.** "Teacher Education In India: Futurological perspectives," *University News*, (May. 28, 1990), pp. 1–7.

**Saha, Sujatha.** "Quality lmprovement of Teacher Education, A Future Perspectives," *University News*, (Sep.13, 1999), pp.6–9.

**Sarup, Anand.** "Basic Issues for Educational Planners," *University News* (Jan.27, 1997).

**———.** "Higher Education Needs a New Paradigm," *University News,* (Jan.27, 1992), pp.1–2.

**Shaik, Mowla.** "Reforming the Existing Education," Education: *The Hindu* (Oct. , 1993), p.19.

**Shanmugasundaram, Yashoda.** "Indian Education From Colonial Tool of Administration to a Strategy of Social Development," *University News*, Vol.37:11, (March 15, 1999), pp. 16–19.

**Sethumadhava Rao.** "Some Thoughts on Planning in Higher Education in India," *University News* (March 8,1993), pp.8–10

**Singh, Karan.** Forward to the *Theory of Education* by M.M.A. Bourai, Delhi: B.R. Publishing Corporation, 1993.

———. "Dimensions of Personality," excerpts from the Convocation Address at the Shivaji University, Koihapur, *University News,* Vol.37:13, (March 29, 1999), pp.20–22.

**Singh, B.K.** "50 Years After: Challenges Facing Teachers," *University News* (Oct.6, 1997), pp.6,7.

**Singh, Amrik.** "Higher Education in A.D. 2000," *University News* (April2, 1990), pp. 1–5.

**Sounderaraj. Francis.** "Curriculum for Colleges in the Twenty-first Century – A Paradigm Francis Shift." *University News* (Sep.27, 1999), pp.1–5.

**Swaminathan, M.S.** "The Knowledge Century," excerpts from the Convocation Addrress At the Karnatak University, Dharwa *University News* (May 31, 1999).

**Takwala, Rani.** "Emerging Perspectives and Paradigms in Higher Education," *University News* (May 19, 1997).

**Tripathi, A.N.** "Ethics and Accountability in the Teaching Profession," *University News* (Jan.24. 1991), p. 1.

**Trivedi, R.S.** "Indian Education and Educators by 2000 A.D.," *University News* (June 14, 1093) pp.3,4.

**Tyler, R.W.** *Basic Principles of Curriculum Instruction:* Syllabus for Education 305, Syllabus Division, University of Chicago Press: Chicago, 1962. pp.22,56.

# Areas of Concern for Inclusion in a Curriculum for Teacher Education, Identified from Opinions of Educationists in Eighty-four Articles between 1990 and 2001*

**I. Area:** *Linkages Between Education and Socio-cultural Development.*

## Objectives

1. Understanding the historical, social, and economic conditions that shaped the higher educational system in India during the British rule.
2. Understanding of factors behind the present pattern of higher education i.e. in the last quarter of the twentieth century, and of changes that have occurred in the system.
3. Awareness of the philosophical, cultural, economic, operational, and managerial constraints and strains on higher education; and how these contribute to immobilization, stagnation, routinisation, adhocism and bureaucratization of educational system, and what the consequences are to the people.
4. Understanding the ways by which education leads to economic growth and self-reliance needed for social development.
5. Understanding the implications of new knowledge and capabilities to micro and macro economic processes, culture and social life: for example, fragmentation of family life, psychotic disorders, and violence.
6. Awareness that bureaucratization and commercialization of education promotes a money-centric attitude to life.

* Bibliography given in Appendix III.

7. Awareness of high correlation between educational levels and expansion of economic and agricultural activities, economic activities in industry and services and land reforms.
8. Awareness of the present and future impact of technology on society's infrastructural, institutional, demographic, and national identity and sovereignty
9. Understanding that privileges will not happen by evolutionary methods but by societal demands.

**II. Area:** *Impact of Socio-culture and Economic Forces on the Educational System and Policy.*

## Objectives

1. Understanding the socio-cultural foundations of education.
2. Awareness that the social outlook that does not promote respect for manual labour, field and farm work, and factory work, supports an educational system promoting white-collar jobs, persisting from McCauley's time.
3. Awareness that the ruling elite's perception of causes of underdevelopment and vision of the future of the society influences the development strategy and the educational policy of the society.
4. Understanding that purism that is not in touch with realities is a cause of most acute crises of relevance
5. Understanding that economy is the base of society, and education is the superstructure and hence to be planned in relation to the economic activities of the society.
6. Understanding that it is utilitarian and pragmatic social milieu that makes teachers partially blind to social commitments, values and ideals.
7. Awareness of sources of crises in higher education, and the correlation of crises in higher education with the economy and social production process.
8. Awareness of the institutional and value framework of our society that is not conducive to fostering excellence.

9. Awareness of factors in the Indian society that leads to wastage of teachers' and students' work hours, time and energy, as for example political or labour strikes and bandhs, inadequate transportation services, and frequent special and religious holidays.
10. Awareness of the policy of considering education as a 'non-merit' item not to be subsidized and of the rejection of this policy as leading to curbing growth of human resources, acculturing existing elitism, obstructing means of self-reliant development , and abandonment of the principles of equity by cutting access to education for all.

**III. Area:** *Social, Cultural, and Economic Changes, the Major Issues They Raise, and the Implications for Educational Policies and the Curriculum in Higher Education*

## Objectives

1. Become aware of the social, cultural and economic changes such as
   a) from tradition to modernity, b. from an industrial to an information society, c. from a welfare state to a liberal market economy, and the issues they raise in the educational system.
2. Become aware of the issues arising from social changes:
   – the appearance of single parent families
   – broken homes, and immigrant families;
   – invasion of western culture in family life and change from tradition to modernity etc., and the implications for education.
3. Become aware of the following major social issues and their implications for educational policies and curriculum:
   a) bringing national integration in a pluralistic society;
   b) the place of secularism and religion in state polity

c) conflict of objectives such as human resource development and environment protection with economic development as an objective,

d) conflict of individual freedoms and planned social order;

e) possessive unrestricted behavior instead of liberation of constructive behavior;

f) conflict of old traditions with new values;

g) rural and urban divide and equality of opportunities in education;

h) the problem of unemployment and appropriateness of investments in education;

i) alienation of educated youth from main stream of society and implications to education received and education needed.

4. Get acquainted with the changing profile of the student population with regard to the diversity of its characteristics, namely:

   Socio-economic conditions, language, religions and culture, mobility, variety of life experiences, educational backgrounds, and levels, needs, learning capacities etc., and implications of these changes to education.

5. Become aware of the increasing demand for education seen in the increasing enrolment of swelling numbers of learners, due to facilities for vocational, liberal, and professional streams multiplying rapidly and getting geographically scattered, and the consequences to the educational system.

6. Become aware of changes in the Indian society that pose new challenges to education such as forces that weaken national and social integration.

7. Understand the relationship between investment in education and employment as in the case of inappropriate or excessive investment causing mismatch between demand and supply leading to unemployment or mismatch between education and

employment, and examine the capacity of our social production system to absorb educated manpower.

8. Realization that a lack of national or global philosophy and of system in regard to education results in educational drift and unorganized expansion.
9. Awareness of the damage done by politicization and commercialization of education, as seen in
   a) nonacademic reasons for new universities,
   b) sacking personnel at will,
   c) unprincipled compromise on issues of merit and quality,
   d) indiscipline and disrespect for law, and
   e) functioning anarchy needing judiciary intervention.

**IV. Area:** *Problems and Deficiencies of the Higher Educational System of India and Remedial Measures*

**Objectives**

1. Awareness of the maladies, problems and defects affecting higher education in Indian universities as pointed out in publications.
2. Awareness of the anachronisms that distort the Indian educational system, consequent to Indian society moving along streams of different ages in agriculture, industry and high technology etc., one blocking speed of development of the other, and the educational policy followed and activities to meet these anachronisms. An example is activities of science and technology of the twentieth century being administered by a system remnant of the nineteenth century.
3. Awareness of major academic malpractices such as:

   misuse of students, neglect of students, academic dishonesty, unfair evaluation practices, unfair awards and appointments, individual unethical practices, immoral character of faculty due to lack of personal integrity and character, reward structure ignoring silent though deserving teachers, rampant caucusism breeding sycophants, and satellites breeding mediocrity, and government support resulting in corrupting money influence in selection of teachers and students.

4. Awareness of factors that contribute to stagnation in the educational system such as apathy, helplessness and hopelessness of academicians.
5. Awareness of the argument that teachers are forced to conform to pervading standards of mediocrity or compartmentalize their life into two parts: one , teaching for a living, and another, for creative work.
6. Understanding that absence of vocational courses and lack of work experience is preparation only for white collar jobs and no sense of dignity of labour; that a narrow focus on knowledge that is not integrated or updated, and exclusion of skills, attitudes and values, in higher education will produce graduates with very little capacity for self-study, poor language and communication skills, a highly limited worldview, and a poor sense of social and national responsibility.
7. Understanding that the lack of academic atmosphere in universities and such qualities as vocational zeal, professionalism, motivation, and commitment and competence in teachers are factors contributing to the poor quality of higher education in India.
8. Awareness of the causes for the poor performance of higher education, other than the above, listed below:
   a) Paucity of resources and inadequacy of input in higher education,
   b) Inadequate infrastructure, funds, and short working days,
   c) Deficiency in relevant skills and knowledge resulting in low productivity,
   d) Wastage of resources seen in unemployment and un-employability of manpower,
   e) Non-implementation of educational policies,
   f) Dilution of standards and absence of standards to follow.

9. Awareness of the opinion that conditions in the educational system render teachers dull, insensitive, uninspiring and paralyze their capacities and desire to perform.
10. Awareness of the opinion that the academic scene in higher education can be described as presenting archaic courses with irrelevant curricula, anaemic syllabus, uninviting instructional materials, unchallenging methods, unreliable evaluation procedures, freezing and de-motivating institutional climate, poor plant facilities, overcrowded classrooms, uncertain schedules, political reasons for stoppage of work and trivial reasons for holidays.
11. Awareness of the opinion that we as a people lack scientific temper and have not yet developed an industrial culture.
12. Understanding that certain built-in barriers such as are against professionalism that act as hurdles in firing inefficient faculty, vested interests, entrenched forces, political and humanitarian considerations, and legal and trade union problems.
13. Understanding that a cause for the hiatus between higher education and real life is that the 'information cargo' dispensed is not relevant to the culture and ethos of the people of the country, and the science and technology we use is of western origin.
14. Awareness of the opinion that no significant evidence is seen in education to prepare our human resources to be competent in terms of world standards in an open market.
15. Awareness of the opinion that the curriculum in higher education is synchretic and not cohesive and has no paradigm of goals.
16. Awareness of the adverse and beneficial impact of technology on education such as:
    a) dehumanizing dimension of technology
    b) limitations of mechanized programmes and teaching machines dominating learning,

c) advent of self-learning technologies such as video packages and programmed learning materials,

d) latest information technologies such as that available in libraries computers, AV equipment, software, photographs, reprographic equipment etc.

17. Understanding that the under-performance of colleges and universities is caused by the closed, direct or autocratic organizational climate of departments.
18. Awareness of the opinion that the academic system in India is extremely rigid and mostly centralized.
19. Awareness of the opinion that administrators lack ability and imagination to enable young teachers utilize their potentiality.
20. Understanding that imposing a homogeneous curriculum on a heterogeneous society, as in the present system, neglects the individual differences in needs and backgrounds depriving them of the benefits of education.
21. Awareness of the opinion that too much weightage is given to research and publications of the teachers at the expense of attention to teaching.
22. Awareness of the opinion that the entrance examination for teaching or the eligibility tests for teaching does not ensure postgraduates who are effective or worthy teachers.
23. Awareness of the opinion that globalization of education, may not be totally beneficial to social progress and cannot take the place of national education for achieving social development in India.

**V. Area:** *Prevailing Socio-educational Context of the Formal Educational System*

**Objectives**

1. Become aware of the alternative parallel and continuing system of education as a context in which formal education is given.

2. Become acquainted with the role and function of such educational advisory bodies as the NICPA, ASC, NCET, SCRT, EMRC, and Textbook Boards set up to improve the quality of higher education.
3. Become acquainted with the philosophical, cultural, economic, operational and managerial constraints that operate on the educational system and how they affect higher education, Some examples are the negative attitude towards manual work due to cultural constraints, ideals of social service replaced by the ides of opportunity cost due to economic constraints and corruption in professions due to philosophical constraints.
4. Understand that the educational system serves a variety of conflicting purpose due to the different participants like the students, parents and political authorities, having no consensus on educational objectives of priority value.
5. Became aware of the alienation of teachers from the higher educational system, as observed by scholars and educational authorities, being caused by the following situations, and think of possible remedies.
   a) Uninterested and unmotivated students aiming only at acquiring degrees and preferring only teachers who help in finding an easy way for doing so.
   b) Having a syllabus prepared by authorities without teachers' participation or contribution of ideas, and inclusion of some approved portions and exclusions of portions considered desirable by teachers.
   c) The system of external examination that gives no feedback to teachers and the lack of trust in the impartiality of teachers in internal evaluation.
   d) Lack of scope for academic discussions and interpersonal contacts among teachers of the same faculty or the same branch of knowledge through formal and informal associations or meetings.

## VI. Area: *Concept and Nature of Education*

### Objectives

1. Understanding of education as an acculturating force, also liberating and empowering if operating in a cultural environment of freedom.
2. Understanding that adequate education will draw its data and inspiration from daily existence.
3. Perceiving education as the manifestation of divinity, dignity and excellence in studies.
4. Realizing that education is value orientation of every learner.
5. Understanding that education is not just transmission of information but also of certain ethical, moral and personal academic values so that wise people use knowledge in their own and mankind's interest is gained.
6. Forming a clear perception of higher education's multifarious roles: social, cultural, economic, political and technological.
7. Realizing the multi-dimensionality of education as seen in the range of objectives such as development of physical, mental and intellectual abilities to learn by oneself from empirical experience and the ability to react in time to changing physical, technical and social environment.
8. Understanding that education is an integral component of human resource development.
9. Understanding that knowledge purified on values becomes wisdom.
10. Understanding that a dimension of education is lifelong learning, and learning as lifelong process.
11. Awareness that developing a holistic view of education at all levels is the desiderata of the day.
12. Understanding that the purpose of education is to move from the level of information to a cultural level, to emancipated level and to self-realization.

**VII. Area:** *Educational Philosophy for Higher Education in India*

**Content**

1. Appreciation of the older Indian ideal according to which those privileged with access to higher education and seek knowledge and truth should give up claim to wealth and worldly power.
2. Belief that we need radical and broad humanism, dynamic secularism and synthesis of material and spiritual values instilled through our educational system.
3. Belief that a university stands for humanism, tolerance, for reason, progress, adventure of ideas and search for truth.
4. Belief that education should broaden the mind to rise above petty sectarian thinking and think about India as a whole to bring about social and national integration.
5. Belief that education stands for creation of a scientific temper seen in the attitude of a search for truth, in cultivation and advancement of frontiers of learning.
6. Understanding that the real danger to society lies in expertise without an integrated wholesome view of life.
7. Understanding that the very foundations of a university are the development of human excellence and pursuit of knowledge, as centers of excellence and relevance.
8. Understanding that to counterbalance the dehumanizing dimension of technology there should be moral and higher traditional values with which modern technology should be harmonized, and a judicious use is made of technology to optimize employment income and productivity, material and life sciences be humanized, developing a humanistic pattern of development.
9. Understanding that the importance of a holistic approach to educational policies help people face conflict, competition and hostility, stresses convergence rather than conflict, cooperation rather than competition.

10. Adopting a multidisciplinary approach in the context of uncertain future, social demands, globalization and technological innovations.
11. Adopting honest eclectism in approach to higher education.
12. Belief that education should show a pro-active role in a changing society by a)being in conformity with the changing educational and social realization b) giving inputs relevant to changing technology and resource constraints c) taking responsibility for providing answers to problems of industry, commerce and other social activities.
13. Holding the opinion that there should be equality of opportunity for higher education, but the right to higher education can accrue only to the gifted, interested, and equality of opportunity should not be deemed ipso facto as equality of achievement.
14. Belief that the aim of higher education is improving the quality of life of the common man, ensuring certain minimum level of quality of life for each citizen in a large population, providing the highest education for at least a few and basic education for all.
15. Upholding the view that students should be indebted to the common man for providing for higher education through his toils and higher education should contribute more through students, compared to the average citizen, to the welfare of the nation.
16. Understanding that education cannot be totally value free as planning of education involves value choices, should promote spiritual, ethical and cultural values and promote the spirit of compassion as a part of Indian ethos.
17. Recognizing that values determine human nature more than the amount of information acquired.
18. Upholding the view that Western models of education should not be imitated thoughtlessly.

**VIII. Area:** *Objectives of Higher Education in India*

**Content**

1. Awareness of expectations from higher education as spelt out in the New Education Policy of 1986: Growth of the GNP, productivity, social development, women empowerment, boosting of modernization and enrichment of the individual.
2. Awareness of minimum national expectations from higher education: a. all round development of potential, b. promotion of standards of excellence through healthy habits and body tuned to perfection, c. preservation and enrichment of indigenous heritage, diversification and reinforcement through science and technology and dissemination of cultural heritage, d. building up a recurrently learning society, self replenishing human resources to promote leadership.
3. Awareness of expectations from investment in education: a. improvement in living conditions of people, b. promotion of social and national integration, c. increase in employment and work opportunities etc.
4. Become acquainted with three kinds of goals for higher education: a. institutional: consisting of the founding philosophy and a mission statement, b. national: expressed in national aspirations, concerns, secular, technological progress and c. global issues.
5. Promote the humanistic approach in education as contained in the following three forms of humanism: theocentric, anthropometric and bio centric as defined by sociologists.
6. Develop attitudes, values and skills that enable the population to learn, adapt and grow, increasing the capacity to learn.
7. Promote academic excellence by meeting the following criteria of indicators of excellence:
   a) an academic atmosphere indicated by academic activities, pursuit of research, number of teaching posts, multidisciplinary courses drafted and taught cooperatively;

b) interaction between departments as a consequence;

c) institutional search for excellence and competition for excellence;

d) manner of appointments of vice-chancellors and teaching staff;

e) standards of university publications as indicated by the status of publishers and reviews;

f) training of good teachers and creative thinkers indicated by new courses being taught and personality of the teachers.

8. Understanding that the real relevance of education lies in: cultivating curiosity. ability to think; acculturating, sensitizing the mind to ethics and aesthetics; and building faith in liberty, equality and fraternity, building faith in justice that transcends sectarian beliefs, reflecting democratic values.
9. Develop the ability to push frontiers of knowledge further and promote production and dissemination of knowledge.
10. Encourage new conjectures, hypotheses and theories, supplement or supplant existing beliefs and help develop new thinking and ability to add own ideas.
11. Awareness of the four kinds of learning stressed in Delors report; learning to know or knowledge, learning to do or ability and skill, learning to live together or value, learning to be or self-realization; and also learning how to learn.
12. Stress on educational principles, application of knowledge to develop capacity to apply knowledge for development leading to skills for occupations.
13. Develop the spiritual center of students, the quest for spiritual maturity, and develop emotional maturity.
14. Encourage critical analysis of our social life, its ideals, values and its institutions, promoting critical thinking.
15. Aim at removal of ignorance, superstition, bigotry and intolerance in our society.

16. Promote awareness of national aspirations and social concerns such as corruption, fundamentalism, inequities, discrimination etc., understanding that higher education is for realization of national and educational goals.
17. Promote values of democracy, egalitarianism, social justice, secularism, excellence, commitment, high performance, cooperation, fellow feeling mutual goodwill and tolerance.
18. Promote understanding of core moral values of our culture for counter balancing the dehumanizing influence of technology; our societal values redefining them in view of erosion of these values.
19. Build awareness of democratic values to be held and foster the democratic values.
20. Sensitize learners to broader concerns and issues in higher education, considering a broader role for education.
21. Get acquainted with the history of disciplines in its broad sense and with the philosophy of the subjects to be taught.
22. Promote the ability to envision the future social and economic and technological situations and challenges to face in professional life.
23. Promote understanding of the ethics involved at the individual and national level in contemporary socio-economic and other issues.
24. Understanding that teamwork and discipline, with a coherent value system is needed to prevent corruption from endangering our economy and polity.
25. Promote understanding of the challenges to socio-economic development in the areas of ecology, economics and gender equity and their educational implications.
26. Promote a positive attitude towards manual labour and uphold the dignity of manual work.
27. Promote development of aesthetic sensibility, perception of beauty, truth and auspiciousness; of creative response to

music, nature and the simple joys of life and environment consciousness.

28. Promote the virtues of compassion and helpfulness, punctuality, discipline. and dedication, teamwork and coordination, paying our debt to society.
29. Aim at rounded personalities, intellectually excellent, socially aware and self-confident, bringing an all round personality development.
30. Aim at making every effort to increase the worth of human resources, such as ability to communicate to students and the community by teaching languages, developing the cognitive faculty of conceptualizing, developing capability for deep thinking leading to rapid achievement of education and the capacity to separate chaff from grain in information.
31. Promote the realization of the supremacy of knowledge in science and technology.
32. Encourage action research and development projects.
33. Address the hyper-consumerism of ultra-promiscuity of horror and violence casting a malign shadow within us.
34. Consider an increased role for education in bringing socio-economic transformation by promoting self-reliance, economic growth, employment, social and national integration, creation of a more equitable society, environment protection, arresting population growth and sustainability.
35. Promote the ability to identify key areas for development of education, and areas of strategic research and teaching.
36. Understand the importance of evolving rules and procedures to prevent abuses and bureaucratic delays in helping educational evolution.

## IX. Area: *Teacher Education Curriculum*

### Objectives and Content

### *A. Teachers roles and tasks*

1. Awareness of the role of improving professional input through action research related to the curriculum.
2. Promoting appreciation of the teacher's role and contribution in improving the quality of higher education.
3. Awareness of the need for change of the passive role of teachers to a pro-active role in policy making and implementation of the policy.
4. Awareness of the multiple roles that teachers should play.
5. Awareness of the university teachers' roles as teaching, consultancy, research and contributing to university decision making.
6. Awareness of the teacher's role as a facilitator, mentor or counselor and as a creative mediator guiding learning.
7. Awareness that without the creative initiative of the teacher, the mental and cultural development of the pupils will be left to chance.
8. Getting acquainted with the characteristics or components of the profession of teaching.
9. Understanding that the teacher's guidance is necessary to explore the topography of the field of an educational endeavor by students and that the teacher should indicate the structure of the field of learning and of the discipline as a creative mediator.

### *B. Development of Teacher's Personality*

10. Utilize opportunities for development of personality, initiative and creativity and also character building.
11. Develop mature dependence on self and be one's own manager to cope with the environment.

12. Cultivate the sense of professional responsibility, especially the particular responsibility to improve upon one's personal and professional competence.
13. Develop intrinsic motivation for pursuing the profession.
14. Promote pride in the profession and the attitude that teaching is a noble profession.
15. Encourage willingness to help and strengthen commitment to academic excellence.
16. Help to formulate criteria of commitment to academic excellence.
17. Promote the ideal of rigorousness in work.
18. Promote creative idealism, a sense of devotion and commitment and also commitment to create a better social order.
19. Develop social sensibility and qualities of altruistic service.
20. Develop sensitivity towards issues of women empowerment and the growing challenge of patriarchy.
21. Promote secular consciousness and qualities of clear thinking, hard work, disciplined application and intelligent and wise leadership.

***C. Acquiring Scholarship***

22. Encourage intelligent interest in subjects studied and taught.
23. Develop awareness of development of one's own specific subject and promote academic depth in the subject.
24. Promote acquisition of the basic foundations of professional knowledge and an adequate understanding of professional and academic terms.
25. Promote study of subjects helpful in facing actual classroom situations.
26. Promote understanding of new concepts such as 'equal opportunity' 'egalitarian social order', 'standards in education' etc.

27. Promote acquaintance with modern means of continuous updating of skills for teachers such as 'distance education', 'virtual classroom', `teleconferencing', 'interactive television' etc.
28. Encourage participation in studies, innovations and experiments.
29. Build understanding of the concept of action research.

**X. Area:** *Educational Practices and Methods*

## Objectives

1. Realize that there is nothing like the best methodology for all subjects, and that teachers and students together can find the best way of handling a subject.
2. Understand that i method of teaching is not simply a product of knowledge but a choice based on assessment of the feasibility and desirability of particular practices in specific instructional settings.
3. Understand the concept of a participative strategy in implementing an educational program, for close observation and rigorous monitoring of classes for objective evaluation and timely feedback for impartial awarding, remediation and punishing.
4. Plan instruction to be learner-centered, reciprocal and responsive to cope with large diverse backgrounds and abilities of learners.
5. Consider the idea of student, teacher and society doing participatory planning of education, and design the broad outlines of courses of studies in consultation with students, filling in the details as they go along with the teaching.
6. Learn to weave assessment into the learning process.
7. Hold the teaching role to be more a mediating role with parallel texts and sub-texts, technology aided instruction, with interactive and independent experiences for students.
8. Consider the practice of the use of teaching assistants to correct assignments.

9. Scrutinize the opinion that increasing the use of media makes teachers lose concern, touch and feel of life in the classroom teaching and the joy of self-expression of the teachers.
10. Understand that innovations to a system need not necessarily be additions to the system but may also be deletions from an existing indolent systems to make it more workable.

**XI. Area:** *Teaching*

**Objectives**

1. Developing contextual pedagogical skills such as competence in teaching, in managing class and the learning process, in evaluation, introducing variety, and in planning or creating learning experiences.
2. Learning what contextual strategies mean and developing the ability to use contextual strategies in teaching.
3. Acquiring knowledge of the psychology of learning and teaching and developing the ability to apply the same in classroom teaching.
4. Promote awareness of systematic approaches in setting educational objectives.
5. Acquiring knowledge of general methods of teaching, acquainting oneself with what is known as the best method and means of teaching a subject, and the use of educational technology in methods of teaching.
6. Awareness of new directions for teaching in higher education.
7. Acquiring and improving basic skills of teaching at college and university levels.
8. Developing skills constituting teacher competence, such as skill in planning and preparing courses of study, innovative teaching, motivating students, enforcing classroom discipline, planning assignments to reinforce teaching, and in evaluation.
9. Understanding that teaching involves diagnostic skill, communication skill, problem solving skill and fine-tuning of such skills.

10. Promote development of broad-spectrum abilities.
11. Bring about realization of the need for innovative teaching.
12. Promote development of ability to create variety and flexibility in classrooms, through ability to use diversified educational methods.
13. Become a multi-skilled worker, understanding that teaching is work of interdisciplinary nature.
14. Develop ability to use methods to arouse the enthusiasm and the curiosity of students.
15. Understand the concept of motivation, acquiring the knowledge of factors and strategies to motivate students to learn, to plan the curriculum and teach in the classrooms.
16. Promote realization of the need for updating efficiency, knowledge in the teaching occupation.

**XII. Area:** *Evaluation*

**Objectives**

1. Become acquainted with the eight goals for external and internal examination as outlined in the New Education Policy of 1986.
2. Become acquainted with the emerging concepts, issues and principles of qualities and quantitative devices for need assessment such as tests, interviews, group discussions, observations, appraisal reports, analysis of learners' answer scripts, etc.
3. Promote the understanding that keeping record of all assignments and quizzes, showing the courses covered as announced in advance, helps evaluation of teaching.
4. Understand that objective, continuous, internal, transparent examination will combat alienation of teachers from students and is considered as good evaluation practice.
5. Examine the reasons and suggest remedies for the opinion held by some that internal examination results in lack of credibility for the degree awarded.

6. Understand the reasons for holding that fair evaluation is by giving grades rather than marks in numerical units, using the normal distribution curve.
7. Understand that good evaluation is continuous, both formative and summative, innovative, lab intensive and through extended contacts, etc.

**XIII. Area:** *The Educational System of India: Structure Organisation and Management*

## Objectives

1. Awareness of the need for coordinating the several subsystems of education vertically and horizontally for promoting mobility and interdisciplinarity in the higher educational system.
2. Examine the need for accountable and autonomous Boards of Education at each level of the educational system of the country.
3. Become acquainted with the role and function of the educational, advisory, supervisory and preparatory infrastructure, namely, NICPA, ASC, NECT, SCET, EHRC, and Textbook Boards, set up to improve the quality of higher education.
4. Understand the merit of the academic calendar being operationalised at the maximum installed capacity of all with reasonable regularity, efficiency and commitment.
5. Become sensitive to inbuilt levers of change.
6. Understand the importance of providing diversified school life with documentary centers, clubs, meeting rooms, leisure centers etc.
7. Examine if structure within the educational system, subjects etc, belie the claims of indigenousness and modernity.
8. Understand the need for quality teacher recruitment to improving the quality of higher education in colleges and universities.

## Chart of Analysis of Four Teacher Roles

Role : Teacher and Counselor
Function : Planning the Curriculum
Tasks (Activities)

A. Planning the Curriculum
   1. Determining Objectives
   2. Organizing the Curriculum( planning learning)
   3. Planning Evaluation ( teaching experiences )

B. Teaching in Class
   1. Arranging Teaching - Learning Situations
   2. Communicating
   3. Supervising and Managing
   4. Evaluating
   5. Decision making
   6. Rearranging Learning Situation

C. Educational Counseling
   1. Preparation
   2. Interview
   3. Follow-up

Role : Scholar
Function : Research
Tasks

A. Research
   1. Selection of Research
   2. Planning of Research
   3. Conducting Research Activities
   4. Evaluation of Research

B. Contributing from Research and Theory to Educational Practices
   1. Selecting Contribution from Research
   2. Field Testing
   3. Recommendation and Adoption of New Educational Practices

Role : Member of Faculty

Function

A. Functional policy Making

Tasks

1. Formulation of Policies, Rules, and Standards
2. Participating in Faculty Meetings and Exercising Membership Rights and Duties,

B. Program Building (Institutional Curriculum Making)

Tasks

1. Providing for Joint Planning with Public on Purposes
2. Study of Overall Purposes and Objectives of School
3. Study of Articulation of Classroom Objectives to School Objectives
4. Sharing in Evaluation of All-school Objectives

C. Administration

1. Record-keeping
2. Decisions on admissions, promotions, detentions, retentions or discharge
3. Coordination of work with Overall Faculty etc
4. Ordering and Maintaining of Technical Equipment

D. Sharing in Non-teaching Responsibilities

Role : Member of Profession

Function

A. Development of Professional Standards and Professional Leadership

Tasks

1. Identifying the educational and Organizational Lacks in the Profession
2. Determining Professional Standards for Leadership
3. Providing Organizational Controls

B. Promoting Professional Self-growth, of Co-professionals and of Prospective Professionals and Practitioners

Tasks

1. Participation in Training and Providing Educational Opportunities for Prospective Teachers
2. Providing Educational Opportunities for Co-professionals
3. Providing Educational Opportunities for Self-growth.

❖ ❖ ❖

## Bibliography of Literature on the Roles of the Teacher


1. **Byrn, D. Led.** *Evaluation in Extension.* United States Department of Agriculture, Federal Extension Service Washington, D. C., 1959.
2. **Campbell, C.** *Current Issues in Higher Education, 1964: Undergraduate Education.* Washington, D. C.: Association for Higher Education, 1964.
3. **Caswell, H.L., and Campbell, D.S.** *Curriculum Development: Theory and Practice.* New York :Harcourt, Brace and World, 1962.
4. **Chandler, B.J.** *Education and the Teacher.* New York: Dodd, Mead and Company, 1961.
5. Commission on *Teacher Competence: Its Mature and Sçone.* San Francisco, Teacher Education Calif.: California Teachers' Association, 1957.
6. **Eckert, R.E.** "Colleges and Universities – *Programs," The Encyclopedia of Educational Research.* edited by C. W. Harris. New York: Macmillan and Company, 1960, P.
7. **Grambs, J.D.** "The Roles of the Teacher," *School and Society.* Edited by H.C. Gross, P.S. Wronski and J.W. Hanson. Boston: D.C. Heath and Company. 1962.
8. **Havighurst, R.** *Becoming an Educator: An lntroduction by Specialists to the Study and Practice of Education.* Boston: Houghton Mifflin Company, 1961.
9. **Justman, J., and Mais, W.A.** *College Teaching: Its Practices and Its Potential.* New York: Harper and Brothers, 1956.

10. **Marble, S.D.** *Current Issues in Higher Education. 1964: Undergraduate Education.* Washington, D.C.: Association for Higher Education, 1964.

11. **Mukerji, R., and Shurnsky, A.** "A Critical Look at the Teacher of Teachers," *The Journal of Educational Sociology General Issue.* 35, No.3 (November, 1961).

12. **Canto, T.N.** *The Dynamics of Learning*, New York: The Dryden Press, 1953.

13. **Sarason, S.B.** et al. *The Preparation of Teachers: An Unstudied Problem in Education.* New York: John Willey and Sons, Inc., 1962.

14. **Smith, E. R.(ed)** *Teacher Education: A Reappraisal.* New York: Harper and Row, 1962.

15. **Stratemeyer, F.** "Changes in Teacher Education: An Appraisal," Symposium on Teacher Education, *Journal of Teacher Education* 14, No.1 (March, 1963).

## Appendix-VII

# Suggestion for a Scheme of Teacher Education, Identified from Literature on Teacher Education

There needs to be various patterns or schemes of teacher education such as full-time courses, part-time courses, self-learning, and inter-institutional specialized courses.

There needs to be general education for building strength of character and openness to new ideas, and specific education for competence in specific jobs. Such general education for preparing college teachers should begin from the undergraduate years.

General and abstract preparation for a profession, apart from direct preparation, widens the vision and develops the power for generalization and abstraction.

Sequential courses in educational theory, practice, policy, methodology and philosophy should be offered.

Prepare a flexible and need-based curriculum, showing the juxtaposition of the social sciences in teacher education.

Evolve a reliable method for relating training with on-the-job performance.

Methods may consist of practicum, mediated self-confrontation, peer teaching, workshop or training modules (use of modular approach for choice in activities)

Assessment of teachers should be suitable to purpose, not restricted to one method, non-threatening, participative, and based on continuous evaluation of both teaching and learning.

There should be orientation to educational research and action research

Establish a mechanism for dissemination of research outcome to teachers and institutions, such as journals and seminars etc.

## Appendix-VIII

# An Illustration of Planning a Motivational Unit as a Starting Point in a Teacher Education Programme

In the following pages an attempt is made to give an illustration of how a teacher educator can plan the introductory session of a teacher education program as a motivational unit. This is a hypothetical plan based on certain assumptions about the student population and the resources of the teacher educator. The illustration shows only one of the ways in which motivation of the students of teacher education may be done. Undoubtedly, feasible motivational plans need to be made by teacher educators for the real life situations taking into account the actual data about the students enrolled in the teacher education program.

### Introduction

The first question for a teacher educator at the beginning of a course in teacher education may well be: "What learning experiences will kindle interest in the prospective teachers in pursuing the course with enthusiasm and faith in benefiting from the course? What will arouse the intrinsic motivation to become effective educators competent to meet the challenges of educating the younger generations!"

Since the prospective college teachers are young adults, one may assume-that they are bound to have needs attributed to this age group. These needs are termed 'growth expansion needs' by psychologists. These needs are listed as need for achievement, power, creativity, self-actualization, broader orientation of role, and also need for social approval and appreciation.[36] While such psychological forces for states of mind may be at a sub-conscious level, more readily felt are some environmental stimuli and expectations of the society with regard to teachers.

An obvious extrinsic motivation would be the desire to get a certificate of a pass in the teacher education program and to get a

Bachelor of Education degree. This would appear important to students since the degree is necessary to get employment in schools or to apply for admission to postgraduate studies in Education, leading to employment in teacher education colleges or departments.

Some knowledge of education as a subject or a B.Ed degree is also needed for appearing for the Eligibility Test for teaching in colleges and universities. Hence the motivation for joining the teacher education program would be chiefly for upward professional mobility. Such students would be more interested in knowing what should be done or learnt to pass the teacher education examinations and would be less concerned with becoming a 'good teacher'.

Students of teacher education come with a background of attitudes, aspirations, and abilities, and a mental 'set' that affect their motivation to learn. Developing these students' intrinsic motivation in education as a subject, against this background, becomes the first challenge to face. The first few sessions and the introductory unit of the teacher education course become a crucial starting point. The learning experiences selected in the beginning for motivating interest in students in their professional education should take into account all the above factors.

Motivating interest in education is an objective that can be reached through meeting one or two intermediary objectives. One such objectives would be 'promoting awareness of the importance of education to social progress and another consequent objective would be 'a realization of the key role of teachers in making education an effective force in social development'. A rationale for these objectives would be that to improve the quality of teachers, an important step is the upgrading of the prestige of the teaching profession.[37]

Reaching the above objectives implies forming a **concept** of the role of education in society and developing a **value** for education as an important force for social progress and for guidance in meeting social problems. Forming a concept of the role of education requires knowledge of the relationship of higher education to development of society by knowing how, and in what ways, higher education in India contributed to social progress in India.

It is expected that when knowledge of thc contribution of education to social development is acquired, also the value for education as an important aspect in social progress will be developed. The step of selecting learning experiences will be, therefore, for achieving the above two objectives. Now the next question will be what learning experiences would lead to achieving the selected objectives. A few learning experiences. are suggested in the following plan for an introductory unit for motivating students to get involved in the teacher education program in which they have enrolled. The unit plan described is only a suggestion, and a limited one, illustrating the concepts of curriculum development and implementation discussed in the chapters of the text.

## An introductory Plan of a Motivational Unit in a Teacher Education Program

*Aim of the Unit*: Motivation of prospective teachers to learn about Education for becoming competent teachers.

*The Major Objective*: Developing value for education as an important force for social progress.

*Intermediary Objectives*: Acquiring an understanding of the relationship of highereducation to the development of a society, and identifying the major social changes in the Indian society that can be attributed to changes in the educational status of the people.

*Specific Objective*

1. Become aware of the changes in the social aspects of the life of your forefathers in the past two generations or so, that improved the quality of life in your generation.
2. Identify which of these changes that brought improvement in the life of your parents and in yours that can be attributed to the education that your parents and grandparents received.

3. Become aware of the social forces and social reformers of India who served as the prime movers' in improving the quality of social life by improving the educational system, during; the nineteenth and twentieth centuries.
4. Become acquainted with the life of outstanding educationists who during the British rule brought about radical changes in the educational system for improving the quality of women's life and for the national development of India.

*The Learning Experiences*

The learning experiences suggested for each specific objective based on hypothetical learning situations in which certain assumptions are made about the resources the teacher educators would be having In the actual teaching situations the resources of the teacher educators are bound to he different. The suggestions for learning experiences are only an illustration of the relationship of the experiences with the learning that is expected to progress towards the attainment of the selected objective.

Learning experiences may range from direct experiences through to simulated classroom experiences, experiments. vicarious audio-visual experiences and abstract reasoning from verbal inputs. Direct experiences may be difficult to provide in a teacher education program for much of the content required to reach the above objectives. Moreover. the prospective teachers who come after graduation may be expected to have some background of experience and knowledge about the social conditions and the social history of India. The leaning experiences suggested here are mostly in the form of readings, group discussions, drawing upon personal experiences and critical thinking.

There are no prescriptions as to how many learning experiences may be planned. Teacher educators would be in a better position to know how many more or less are necessary. Though an attempt has been made to list the learning experiences to move from the more concrete. familiar and simpler levels to higher levels and more complex aspects, the lasting is a suggestion and open to change, as there is no research basis for it except a logical one.

## Chart of Sessions of Learning Experiences for Each Specific Objective

*Specific Objective*

1. Awareness of changes in the social aspects of the lives of our fore-fathers that led to improvement in the quality of life later.
2. Awareness of the influence of education on social change:

| | *Learning Experiences* | *Resources* |
|---|---|---|
| a) | Discuss in small groups what aspects of the social and family life changed as far as could be recalled in each one's history. | Families of those accessible to students through informal interviews |
| b) | Make intelligent guesses as to which changes can be set down to the influence of education forefathers received. | |
| c) | Write about changes in their own family living practices that each student felt were due to education they received. | if accessible, family diaries and family albums. |
| d) | Write a brief essay on how the educational system of India, as you know it, benefits the Indian society. | |
| e) | Get an idea of how much or how little the Indian educational system contributed to social progress in the Indian society in the opinion of | Recommended readings on this topic distributed by the instructor. |

| Learning Experiences | Resources |
|---|---|
| scholars in Indian Education and Sociology. | |
| f) Choose any specific social change for the better in our neighborhood or community or town that you have come across either personally or through the media, and try to trace its beginning, causes and hurdles faced. Examine the education of the youth had helped or hindered or had no part in it, and how much external forces were involved such as politics. industry, economic and social reforms. Share this report with others in class sessions for discussions. | Newspapers, journals, TV and radio broadcasts and personal observation. |

This session may extend over ten or more days with the class meeting daily for a few hours for group discussions and exchange of' results achieved.

Evaluation of the involvement of the students needs to be done by the teacher educator The likely evidence of involvement may be found in increasing voluntary participation by students in class meetings and the quality of written work done. As far as possible the resources for study should he made available to students.

## Second Session

3. *Specific Objective:* To become aware of the social forces and social reformers of India who served as the 'prime movers' in improving the quality of social life by improving the educational system. during the nineteenth and twentieth centuries.

| *Learning Experiences* | *Resources* |
|---|---|
| a) Become acquainted with the bio-graphies of at least two eminent reformers of India who were respon-sible for a notable reform in the social life of the people. Note their personality characteristics and the means they used to motivate people to change their attitudes and social practices. Note what kind of educational preparation the reformers received and if they used the educational approach in their reform movements | Biographies of several social reformers to be made available in the library. Films are to be made available |
| b) Be informed as to the educational methods eminent social reformers used to motivate people to change | |
| c) What educational reforms were brought about by social reformers to motivate social changes already taking place? Question to be answered by gathering information from readings given by instructor. | Readings list of relevant books prepared by the instructor. |

4. *Specific Objectives:* Become acquainted with the life of outstanding educationists who during the British rule brought about radical changes in the educational system for improving the quality of women's life and for national development in India.

| | Learning Experiences | Resources |
|---|---|---|
| a) | Discuss in groups the influence each eminent educationist like Rammohan Roy. Karve. Vidyasagar and such personalities had on improving social life, and whether on a smaller scale even less known average educator can influence the community through their students. | Books on the achievements of eminent social and educational reformers. |
| b) | A panel discussion with reputed statesmen, educators, social reformers and educational administrators on the role of the teacher and importance of teachers in uplifting the society. | Interview with a senior reputed teacher with respect to the satisfaction to he gained in teacher's professional life. |

## References Cited


[1] Brubacher, *Op.cit.*, p.20

[2] Ibid., pp. 21, 22.

[3] Ibid, p.42.

[4] Ibid, p.72

[5] Ibid, p.95,

[6] Ibid, pp. 119,120.

[7] Ibid, p.144.

[8] Ibid, p.164.

[9] Ibid, p.187.

[10] Ibid, pp. 220, 230, 289.

[11] Ibid, pp. 308, 309.

[12] Ibid, pp. 348, 349.

[13] Allchin R, and Bridget, The Birth of Indian Civilisation: India and Pakistan Before 500 B.C. (Hammomdsworth, England: Penguin Books Ltd., 1968), pp.100–125.

[14] Ibid, pp.127–144.

[15] Ibid, *Loc.Cit.*

[16] Radha Kumud Mookerjec, *Glimpses of Ancient India*: Chapter II, edited by K.M. Munshi and R.R.. Diwakar, Bharatiya Vidya Bhavan : Bombay, 1960. pp.12–19.

[17] G. Feuerstein, S. Kak and D. Frawley, *In Search of the Cradle of 'Indian Civilisation.* Motilal Banarsidass : Delhi, 1999. Chapter 3, pp.45–49.

[18] Mookerjee Op.Cit.,pp12-19

[19] K.M. Sen Hinduism: The World's Oldest Faith (Penguin Books: Hammondsworth, 1965) pp.69–71.

[20] Ibid, p.74

[21a] Ibid, p.72.

[21b] 1bid, pp. 79–81.

[21c] Ibid, pp. 81, 82.

[21d] Ibid. pp. 82,83.

[21e] Ibid. pp. 83, 84.

[22] Sen, *Op.cit.*, pp. 90–96.

[23] Nilkanta Sastri, *Op.cit.*, pp. 54, 55

[24] Ibid, p. 173.

[25] Ibid, p.224

[26] G. Manickkavasagam, Commentary for the *Kural*, Madurai : Aruna Press, 1966. p.85.

[27a] Nilkanta Sastri, *Op.cit.* p.305

[27b] Ibid, 306

[28a] Sen, *Op.cit.*, pp. 93, 94.

[28b] Ibid, pp. 95, 96.

[29] Ibid, pp. 97–100.

[30] Ibid, pp. 100,101.

[31] Ibid, pp.103–107.

[32] Romila Thapar,_*A History of India: Vol.I* Penguin Book Ltd. Delhi, 1965, p.172

[33] P.N.Jungawalla, *Human Values in Zoroastrian Religion,* (Bharatiya Vidya Bhavan, Bangalore, 1998) pp. 11–27.

[34] Kabir, *Indian Philosophy of Education*, Asia Publishing House: New Delhi, 1961), pp. 189–192.

[35] Genda Singh, *A Brief Account of the Sikhs.* Amritsar: Siromani Gurudwara Prabandak Committee.

[36] Kuhlen., Supra, chapt. Vl, p.116

[37] J.S. Bruner, *The Process of Education.* (Cam. Mass.: Harvard University Press, 1962). p.89.